Tom Corkery's Dublin

TOM CORKERY'S DUBLIN

ANVIL BOOKS

First published 1980 by
Anvil Books
90 Lower Baggot Street Dublin 2

ISBN 0 900038 53 1

Typesetting Computertype Limited
Binding J. F. Newman Limited
Printed in the Republic of Ireland
by Cahill Printers Limited

CONTENTS

PHOTOGRAPHS

The articles in this book were written in the late 1940s and 1950s. Most of the photographs were taken in the same period. An occasional later photograph is included where the setting has not changed appreciably in the meanwhile.

We gratefully acknowledge the enormous assistance given to us in tracking down these old photographs by The Irish Times (who very generously made their files available to us), George Duncan and Bord Failte.

Everything finally flows into O'Connell Street

Prologue

Dublin

Dublin is not, thank Heaven, a queen among cities.   Rather is she a garrulous pleasure-loving provincial lady of good family, settling comfortably into middle-age, putting on too much weight in the wrong places. There is enough malice in her to keep her conversation interesting, and hospitality is for her more a pleasure than a duty. Like all provincial ladies she loves the fuss of visitors; she will flatter them to their faces, gossip about them behind their backs, and is as much flattered as annoyed if, when they leave, they make snide remarks about her. The only unforgivable thing is to say nothing at all about her.

An old bag of words, but mother and foster-mother of some famous sons and with no intention of letting you forget the fact. She will never tire of showing you where her James used to walk, recalling what her Sean used to say, how her Willie and George and Oscar used to behave; she will breathe her George Bernard down your ear until you scream for mercy. And she will blandly forget that when she had them she used to clip their ears every time they opened their mouths. But you cannot help liking the loquacious old dame, with her long-winded reminiscences and her sentimental keepsakes all over the drawing-room. Whatever her failings parsimony is not one of them; dinner or no dinner, she dines at seven.

Her mornings are still elegant, not too harsh, not too obtrusive. There is not too much rattle, not too much clangour; a gentle susurration, the gently refined invitation to be up and about. If sirens call they do so in muted half-hearted fashion, as though they are apprehensive of being prosecuted for disturbing the peace, and church bells interpolate occasional reminders that not by bread alone doth man live. People stop and talk to each other, maybe not too worried whether they get to their work on time. Indeed, one suspects, quite a few do not make it at all.

NOT TO WORRY. It is the real motto of the town, the explanation of its haphazard growth, and of its survival throughout a thousand years of very worrying history. For Dublin's was not a natural birth; the Danes who established it did so, not as the capital of Ireland but rather as a defence against Ireland. Nor did it have a natural growth, as normal towns grow; rather did it erupt and expand at irregular intervals in a series of fitful convulsions.

For six centuries it stayed put on its hill around and beyond Christchurch, while its Norman occupiers occupied themselves in building bigger and better walls. Then in rapid succession came the Duke of Ormonde and seventeenth-century expansion north of the river, eighteenth-century granite and Palladian, followed by Georgian red-brick, nineteenth-century factories any old place, and twentieth-century suburbs all over the place.

Because of this piecemeal progress you cannot just walk the town looking for its historical glories in neat packaged areas. Matters of high architectural interest are not exactly set out for you; they crop up at you from the most unlikely places. You look down a rather dubious river, up a dingy quayside, and you experience the full majesty of the Four Courts. You turn out of the desolation of North King Street into Blackhall Place and encounter the chaste, withdrawn facade of the former King's Hospital (the Bluecoat School). You walk up the most regrettable Constitution Hill, to be greeted by the green sward and classic lines of the King's Inns. How in heaven's name, you ask yourself, did these things ever *get* where they are?

There is so much of Dublin that can only be sped through with the passing tribute of a sigh. But for that, the surprises when they come are all the more piquant. Off the slattern High Street a turn down the steps under St. Audeon's leaves you standing under the old walls of the Norman town. Across the river you walk through rows of red-brick artisans' dwellings to be confronted with the Norman tower of St. Michan's, where owing to some unique preservative in the air of the vaults the bodies of long-buried men from the Crusades on are preserved. You sit in the friendly little green oasis of St. Patrick's Park, with on one side the lancet windows and flying buttresses of St. Pat's Norman Gothic, and on the other the red-brick, the curlicues, the pediments, porticos, pillars and what-have-you-not of the rococo Victorian Iveagh Trust Building. It is a contradiction to delight by its very impertinence.

Contradiction is perhaps the operative word for Dublin. Nothing leads on to what one would reasonably expect. Behind the neon glitter of O'Connell Street lie decaying demolished tenements, storage sheds, empty spaces. Off Henry Street's fashionable shopping stores run ancient rickety little streets on their way to the Liffey. Over the classical granite of Gandon's eighteenth century Custom House looms the towering glass and concrete of Scott's twentieth-century Bus Station, the only connection between them being that they were both planned against the wishes of the citizenry, raised to a chorus of derision from the citizenry, and completed to the ecstatic admiration of the citizenry . . . that is the form of the city, and the form of the citizens.

The river is Dublin's great dividing line; south is for the most part native; north is more often what came in on the boat or train. South is a confederation of little independent enclaves, each one possessing a distinctive character of its own. You start with Inchicore, the railwayman's town. Beyond it sprawls the warren of twisty hilly lanes, ancient cottages, barracks turned into living quarters and tinkers-up-for-the-week that form the scenery of Mount Brown and Kilmainham. Next is James Street and hinterland, Guinness town, acres and acres of it, where rail tracks traverse cobbled streets and the air is full of brewers' smells. A few steps west and you are into the ancient Liberties of Dublin, stretching south to Pimlico and Newmarket, where you find echoes of history around every corner; memories of Dean Swift, the Huguenot weavers and the faction-fighting Liberty Boys.

Typically this toughest of Dublin's quarters is closely adjoined by Dublin's fashionable quarter of Grafton Street. Land of pubs *à la mode*, exclusive shops, restaurants where you eat in French, students, beautiful women, art, overeating, overdrinking, big talk and small thinking. A few more steps, and the bookshops, the chatter, the tinkling coffee cups have vanished, while you wander through the decorous Georgian territory of Fitzwilliam and Merrion, hushed sanctuary of museums and medical men and Ministers of State, where a footfall is by day an intrusion, by night an offence. Further out the tall elegant suburbs of the Pembroke estate make noble monuments to the halcyon days when Suburbia had servants, while a little distance away on the estuary of the Liffey, are the fishing and docking villages of Ringsend and Irishtown, a republic so self-contained that a local marrying a 'city-girl' can still be reprimanded for bringing 'the black foreigner' into his home.

North Dublin has fewer of these little self-sufficient enclaves. Its Gardiner Georgian has vanished or decayed, its once famous low-life quarter of Monto has been levelled. One quarter just seems to flow into another quarter and everything finally flows into O'Connell Street, where the big cinemas, the juke-box cafes, the neon, the ice cream saloons and the crowded pavements make everybody somebody but no one anybody.

There are exceptions of course. Parnell Square at night with its dance halls, ceilí halls, committee rooms, trade union headquarters, does have a pulse of its own. Smithfield still carries a faint dying odour of horses and hay. Stoneybatter and Oxmantown still considers itself cattle country, and its people are still called cowboys. Ballybough away north on the Tolka has a life of its own and still remembers when it was Mud Island and all its inhabitants

Mud Islanders. But apart from these north Dublin is strictly Big Town and Main Street, and no social distinctions.

Not indeed that there is any real social snobbery in Dublin. But south of the river there are little social distinctions, and a true Inchicore man would feel as uneasy in a Duke Street public house as would a Fitzwilliam man in Inchicore. Still, even if the race-course tout from the Liberties can roll a much thicker wad of notes than the intellectuals from Anne Street, he does not necessarily scorn the poor devils on that account. The town is too small for that kind of carry on. We all have relations in the Government; we all have relations in jail.

Among Dubliners argumentation will flow for hours as to what exactly constitutes a true Dubliner. Historically the Dubliner is like his own native coddle, a stew cooked for a long time from many varied ingredients. Gael and Norseman; Norman soldier and burgher of Bristol; French Huguenot and Flemish refugee; men from the plains to the West and men from the mountains to the South; sailors home from the sea and soldiers from the wars returning; these are the ingredients. The end-product is salty, continually on the boil.

And yet perhaps the most striking attribute of the Dubliner is his apparent indifference to the march of time, combined with a bland imperturbability in the face of threatened disaster. It may be perhaps that you are a financier arranging a merger that could beggar you overnight or a politician waiting for an election count that could put you into Limbo for evermore. But if, at the climax of your anxiety, you can still stroll down O'Connell Street at the pace of a languid tortoise, nodding blandly to acquaintances left and right and stopping to inspect every diversion in your path, then you are a true Dubliner, and the town will stop to do you honour.

'Thar he goes,' the citizens will proclaim ecstatically in your wake. *'Thar he goes, and in spite of all his trouble thar's not a bother outa him'.*

Not to show a bother outa you then is the first prerequisite of a Dubliner. The second is to have a lively tongue in your head. If we ever try to symbolise Dublin in a statue it will have to be of a man talking. The only statues that we have not blown up are of men talking . . . Grattan, Moore, O'Connell, Father Matthew and Parnell (Nelson survived for years in his capacity as traffic director and because nobody could devise a means of getting at him.)

When we cannot find anybody left to listen to our talk, we either start talking to ourselves, emigrate to Hyde Park speakers' corner or write plays. In Dublin bus-conductors write plays; so do policemen, priests, taxi-drivers, painters, politicians, plumbers, professors, publicans, earls, students, civil servants, bank clerks, housewives, school-teachers and school children. Those

A provincial lady settling comfortably into middle-age

who have not the patience to write plays, act in plays. We have an annual festival of theatre which is really an annual festival of talk. Most of our television programmes consist of men talking at other men and the secret desire of every one of us is to be one of the talkers. The only Dublin man in history who was ever content to sit and listen was James Joyce and, as everybody now knows, he finally got his own back.

The Dublin social, as distinct from the cultural, scene is very varied. It goes on all the year round and ranges from art exhibitions to horse racing to literary festivals via medical and scientific congresses. It is not to say of course that these grave and learned conventions of the arts and sciences are designed by their organisers as social binges; it is only that they invariably end up that way. And for all her visitors the city changes its face; high-spirited in an aristocratic way for Horse Show Week, jovial in a robust manner for returning American Gaels and GAA finals, hail-fellow-well-met for the rugby internationals, long-haired and longer-winded for the theatre festivals.

You are quite likely to meet anybody you know at a Dublin festival. Anybody that is except the Dublin man. For the Dublin man does not go to rugger; he does not go up to the executive suites of high society or down to the vaults of St. Michan's; he does not go to the Ballsbridge horse shows and he does most of his horse racing in the bookmakers' betting offices. His city is run by men from the south; his finances are run by men from the north; his multiple stores are run by men from God-Knows-Where. Standing solidly by his own street corner, monarch of all he chooses to survey, the Dublin man looks blandly, ironically, imperturbably at his masters and his festivals, sometimes, only sometimes, wondering as he views the changing scene if he is not in danger perchance of becoming the only real stranger in the strange new city growing up around him.

A seemly and decorous interior in shades of brown and mahogany

The Pint

Pintmanship

One regrets to have to mention it, but of recent times a certain frivolous approach to the drinking of the pint is becoming manifest. Much of the trouble is no doubt due to the change in the social status of the pint. Once the pint was solely the fodder of spit-and-sawdust citizens who understood it and who knew how to treat it. It was rarely observed in polite society except maybe in the paw of some recognised eccentric. But today, all sorts of élite hostelries are dishing it out, and all sorts of élite citizens are lapping it up.

That is the situation that gives one to pause. To no man does one grudge the pint; but one must deprecate the false-hearty and the chi-chi habits which in certain quarters of late are becoming associated with its consumption. The pint of stout was never intended for the palate of the kind of ruffian who would dilute its creamy thickness with lesser but more potent fluids. Much less is it suited to be sloshed about or raised aloft in beer-mugs with handles to them, as though it were no more than a sort of black ale. Stout, unlike ale, is not a hail-fellow-well-met beverage. It is a sensitive and delicate liquor, easily upset. Unlike ale, it takes time to settle, and once settled should not be unduly disturbed.

One speaks of the pint of stout because if one is going to drink stout one should be prepared to face up to it in its proper measure, the pint measure. To see stout confined in a half-pint glass is a sad sight, like having to look at a lion in a monkey's cage. Nothing less than a pint measure is adequate to contain the massive majesty of stout, to proclaim its sombre dignity.

It should be remembered that the pint of stout is a dignified drink for dignified men. The poet Yeats once referred, in a most unfortunate phrase, to 'porter-drinkers' randy laughter', and one frequently encounters young citizens today acting under the impression that if they are not being 'randy' with their pints they are not being quite right. Nothing could be further from the truth. A true pintman is never boisterous in the presence of his pint; when he condescends to laugh at all, it is with a deep, slow, ruminative, rumbling sound, counterpointed by satisfied gurgling internal noises.

The true pintman always approaches his pint with reverence, 'in a contemplative fashion, and a tranquil state of mind'. He knows that the pint is a contemplative drink, to be contemplated as well as to be drunk. The true pintman does not even need to be in company when he has his pint before him, for his pint is his company. If you study the good pintman in a pub you will observe how he can stand (no pukkha pintman ever sits) staring into his glass for long periods, thinking deep thoughts. This is because he knows that truth lies at the bottom of his glass, or if not that glass the next one, or, at the very most, the one after that. So he is always unhurried in his drinking habits (it is only plain-porter dockers and silly-billy students who swallow their pints at one swig), and when finally he does condescend to speak it will be invariably with wisdom, if not always, alas, with perfect enunciation.

To be a good pintman it is essential that one's first step should be a step in the right direction; i.e., the direction of a good pint house. The essentials of a good pint house are: (1) a good cellar, insulated from extremes of heat and cold; (2) a dedicated landlord; (3) a regular and knowing clientele; (4) an absence of ale-quaffers, gin-sippers, whiskey-suppers, or wine-bibblers; (5) a seemly and decorous interior in shades of brown and mahogany, relieved only by the glitter of glass; (6) a counter of marble or mahogany, sufficiently high to permit that a man, resting his left foot upon the foot-rail and his left elbow on the top of the counter, should be almost at eye level with his pint; (7) sawdust. Framed enlargements of hurlers, footballers, horses or dogs are in keeping with both the pint and the pintman's interests; partitions are useful, protecting the superior pintman from the intrusions of more vulgar drinkers; and there should, ideally at any rate, be an absence of carpets, plush, fancy little tables, women, piped music, or anybody under the age of twenty-one.

In a good pint house it is not necessary to specify one's drink. No matter how many drinks may be on display behind the counter there will never be more than the one sacred drink atop of the counter. So it is sufficient to manifest oneself and the barman will immediately start reaching for the pump handle.

If he is a good barman he may take anything up to five or six minutes before his stately ceremony of pumping, re-pumping, scraping, levelling, topping, is completed. During that period one should remain discreetly in the background, trying to give the appearance of a person in a trance or a coma. It is the very *apogée* of impertinence to betray either impatience or curiosity during the course of the ceremony. When your pint is ready the barman will call you: *'Now Mister B . . .'* if he knows you by name, or . . . *'Wan Pint A Stout Coming Up . . .'* if he does not.

When your pint comes up it will come up thick and creamy, in a plain glass

A regular and knowing clientele

tumbler without a handle to it. Its substance will be such that (in the words of the *cognoscenti*) 'you could take a knife and fork to it'. There will be no need to worry about its quality; the very walls of a pint house would fall down if a poor pint was served.

Most pintmen have their favourite houses to which they go regularly. But they frequently have to go travelling none the less, for every pintman secretly lives in dread of the thought that somewhere—it might be some new luxury pub in a new luxury suburb, or it might be an ancient old house down some forgotten back street—there exists a pint better than the pints he knows. To have such a place mentioned by another in his presence and not to be able to discourse upon it would be to the pintman the ultimate disgrace.

It is necessary, then, before one reaches the stage of superior pintmanship to have travelled around a bit. The wider the range of houses to which one has travelled the more authority one can claim. And here, unfortunately, lie the pitfalls for the unwary. For it is a sad fact that not every house treats the pint with the respect due to it. There are places where the barmen, if they judged you a tyro, would slap up a pint at you in ten seconds. There are other barmen who, by some magical formula of their own, can pull a pint in such a manner as to make it taste like dishwater. To pull a pint like this is a crime against one of the world's great drinks. To accept it is to become an accessory after the fact.

It behoves the pintman then, whenever he enters a strange house, to adopt a critical attitude, and to let everybody concerned see that they are in the presence of a critic. One should approach the counter with an inquisitorial air, trying to look like an inspector of something or other. When the pint is served to you it should be allowed to rest for a minute on the counter. Then it should be embraced firmly with the fist, raised gently to the lips, and tasted. If there is any taint of sourness the barman should be assaulted forthwith.

If there is no sourness then one may proceed to the next test. For this, one should take a swig of such proportions as to lower appreciably the level of the stout in the glass. The glass should be held towards the light. If it is a good pint a close-textured curtain of creamy froth should be clinging to the glass surface of the emptied part of the tumbler, with an even thicker ring of froth encircling the circumference of the tumbler at the former level of the pint. With every further swig a further ring of froth should be clearly discernible on the glass. If, after you have finished your drink, your emptied tumbler is as ringed as a zebra, then you have had a good pint, and the best compliment you can pay the barman is to have another one.

In many years spent in pursuit of the perfect pint I learned, from a friend of mine, the best method of ensuring that the barman does his best to achieve it. He is a very large man, this chap, with a face that in its time has launched a thousand battles and a disposition (until mellowed at about his sixth pint) somewhat akin to that of the late Genghis Khan.

Entering a strange house my friend always moves directly to the counter. He never has to wait for counter space; it always seems to become immediately available to him. Then, mesmerising the nearest barman into immediate attention, he leans his massive frame across the counter . . .

'A Pint A Stout,' he begins; and as the barman reaches for the pump handle, '. . . FOR DRINKING.' he concludes.

I have never heard of him getting a bad pint yet.

This, then, is pintmanship in the true sense. It is inexpensive, rewarding to the body, soothing to the soul, and leads one into long, pleasant and philosophic conversations. There is no problem of art, morality or world politics that cannot be solved by a group of good pintmen in the course of an evening's session.

There is only one thing more to remember; great pintman are born, not made. One may envy a great pintman his capacity; one may even wonder where he puts it all; but one should never try to emulate him. Discover one's capacity and stick to it. The pint is a friendly drink, in no way treacherous, and will not harm those who treat it right. It is in a sense our National Drink, and has indeed quite a similarity to most of us, being large, black, thick, big-headed, slow to come up, and slower to settle down.

Is it any wonder that we like it so?

'A pint a stout . . . for drinking'

People

Blowing out the Paycock

The way things are going today we are in grave danger of losing one of our most unusual and picturesque citizen-types. I mean the ubiquitous fellow who always seems to be standing at every street corner, large mouth hanging open, long nose stuck up in the air, an amiable vulture eternally hovering for his scraps of gossip and his carrion of accident, seeing all, knowing all, and telling all. In the words of his butties he is a 'mouth'; in the minds of his fellow citizens a waster; in the heart of the tourist a 'charachter', and in the figures of the economist a non-productive unit.

You can always distinguish the non-productive unit from his fellows at the corner, because while they come and go in accordance with the employment rate—if they are honest—or police activity—if they are not—the non-productive unit never goes. He fits into his street corner like a sort of indigenous plant that has grown up somehow out of the pavement, and the place would look undecorated without him.

The weather never bothers him, hail or sun. He hocks his jacket in winter to redeem his overcoat; he hocks his overcoat in summer to redeem his jacket. The duodenal ulcer knows him not; hardened arteries and nervous disorders pass him by; and when busy citizens hurrying by on their way to the acquisition of these things see him standing there—half mystic, half oracle—they get apoplectic with rage, and start muttering about how maybe Hitler had the right idea after all.

Now he is in the process of being, as he himself would put it, 'blown out', and the two modern developments that are blowing him out are the emergence of the Planned State, and the revolt of the lady he calls his 'oul' bird'.

The Planned State does not take kindly to the idea of a citizen who cannot be given a specific function and placed in a proper category. A man standing at a street corner is a standing reproach to the Planned State, and, if it cannot make him work, it insists, at the very least, on giving him a proper bench in a hygienic park and making him sit on it.

But benches in parks are not part of the life pattern of the Dublin drone. He is not like his Latin counterpart, a sleeper. He likes to be where the action is; where accidents are happening, so that he can explain whose fault it was. He is the man who always takes the injured party to hospital, rescues the cat from off the burning roof, pulls the chisler out of the river. And a State that does not envisage situations where cats have business on roofs or chislers have business in rivers has no need of these services.

Even so, while the drone might be able to resist the attack of the Planned State, there is nothing he can do about the revolt of his oul' bird. No man can afford to be a drone these days without the active support of his oul'bird. She is the one who sells the fruit at one street corner while he holds up the other. It is of her he speaks when, at the end of the long day's standing, he shakes himself, looks down towards the boozer and mutters to the boys: 'I think I'll mosey across to the Oul' Bird and touch her for a few shillings . . .' And now, after years of happily functioning as his provider, the oul' bird has revolted. Juno has blown out the Paycock, and his world has truly come to a terrible state of chassis.

It is the cinema and the pulp magazine that have caused the revolution. Between them they have brought the oul' bird into contact with a civilization where Paycocks are bad news, and are referred to, not as 'charachters' but as hobos. She herself has not yet reached the stage where she would demand of him that he actually sweat his brow, but she has learned that a fur coat is warmer than a shawl, and that port in a lounge bar is more 'respectable like' than porter in a snug. That is why today you see less Paycocks standing at corners, and more men carrying crates from the market for their oul' birds. They carry the crates or they go thirsty.

There is only one other thing left to save the non-productive unit from extinction, and that is the increasing necessity for the queue in modern living. When the January sales get under way, the oul' bird likes to be top of the queue, and for that purpose there is no more untiring stand-in than the drone. For him, the matter is merely one of changing the time and place of his stance, and no politician ever elected has faced the prospect of an all-night sitting with more equanimity than the drone can face an all-night standing in Talbot Street on a cold January night.

You will observe him when there is a shortage of anything anywhere. He is first on the queue outside the O'Connell Street cinemas. He is up at the crack of dawn when there are tickets for the big match on sale. He does not buy nor does he sell, for the only commercial transactions he understands are the purchasing of pints and the writing out of complicated bets for bookies' offices. He just holds the ring for the spiv. We pass him by, wondering what possible contribution he can be said to make towards the preservation of our values. But he goes on looking down his long nose at us, for in his heart of hearts he believes, to paraphrase the poet, that he is the value we are working to preserve.

Us Jacks and our Bit of a Nark

A barney of some kind was in progress at the corner of Cole's Lane and Parnell Street, and local citizens, attracted by the noise, were, with much tumult and hilarity, forming themselves into what the District Court, in its curiously morose way, terms A Disorderly Scene.

The immediate cause of the disturbance it appeared had been a collision between two citizens, one with a hand-cart of old clothes, the other leading a horse-dray full of iron bedsteads. Around them the crowd had gathered in a large circle, tumbling and swaying with the tactical moves of the combatants. At intervals, oul' wans, the front line correspondents of all these affairs, would appear on the perimeter and screaming estatically . . . 'They're pourin' blood . . . the pewer fellas, there's murder goin' on . . . they're sphoutin' . . . they'll kill each other . . .' disappear as quickly again into the vortex.

I was debating whether or no to see the thing to its conclusion, when a refined voice spoke in my ear.

'I say,' said the voice, 'should we not try to do something before harm occurs? This begins to assume the aspect of a very ugly scene.'

I turned in amazement to observe a genteel-looking person standing beside me. An Englishman possibly, or a resident of some southside suburb, innocent of our centre-city pastimes and removed from undue contact with the hoi-polloi.

'I think,' I began to explain gently, 'that you misunderstand the basis of the affair. This is not a fight; it is a pastime, and for Dubliners born between Pimlico and the Diamond it is the National Pastime. We call it,' I explained. *'Having a Bit of a Nark.'*

'Not a fight?' asked the Englishman.

'Certainly not!' I replied, 'Rather is it a form of folk-drama, with the actors making up their lines as they go along, and,' I elaborated, 'in this city of Sheridan, Shaw and O'Casey, where every man is his own dramatist, a high dramatic intensity can often be achieved by real experts with a remarkably small flow of blood. If you would care,' I invited, 'to take a closer look?'

We got to the front in time for a beautiful moment of crisis. Old Bedsteads had just pushed Old Clothes in the chest.

'I'm tellin' ya now! I'm warnin' ya! Stop yer humpin' pushin',' declaimed Old Clothes; and then, overexcited by his own ringing lines, so far forgot himself as to grip his opponent by the arm.

It was, of course, a shockingly bad tactic, giving Bedsteads a splendid opportunity of taking front and centre with his own histrionics.

The opportunity was not lost. Bedsteads gazed, petrified with horror, at Old Clothes' hand: 'Take yewer hand offa my arm.' he choked.

Old Clothes tried to bluster but Bedsteads was not to be upstaged: 'TAKE YEWER HAND OFFA MY ARM,' he roared.

It was a tense moment. If Old Clothes were to remove his hand he would perforce lose face with the crowd. If on the other hand he were to retain his grip he would force his opponent to the unthinkable stage of direct or even forceful action, and be deemed clumsy by the audience. For such moments, however, are the great dramatist-actors born.

For Old Clothes did not exactly remove his hand from his opponent's arm. No: With an alchemy of movement too exquisite to describe he permitted, as though he were a king bestowing a favour, *his opponent's arm to fall from his grip.* There was a mingled gasp of admiration and relief from the audience.

I turned in triumph to the Englishman. 'There,' I said. 'You see what I mean.'

But he still could not see . . . 'Chap's yellow surely.' he complained.

I could do little but give him a withering look, for now the great climax was approaching. From his end Bedsteads had noted the arrival of two reliable butties, experts in the craft of holding back a man from his opponent. Suddenly, as though tried beyond endurance, he threw his coat on the ground and rushing with puissance and panache at Old Clothes was hauled back dead on schedule, inches short of his objective, by his remonstrating butties.

Old Clothes was in a like happy position. His wife had just arrived and, screaming wildly, had proceeded to wrap herself around him. Now he too could go all out in safety and, roaring like a bull, he hurled himself and his struggling wife across the ring, closely followed by oul' wans, chislers, messenger boys and all the dogs in the street.

I turned to the Englishman. 'This looks like the end,' I said apologetically, and watched as both parties, stumbling, struggling and roaring threats, gradually separated, one spilling into Henry Street, the other breaking up into numerous discussion groups in Cole's Lane. From somewhere a large and placid Garda had appeared and, with infinite dexterity, having first chained his bicycle to the nearest railing, was simultaneously reproving oul'

wans, directing motorists, cuffing chislers and kicking dogs out of the way.

I walked up Henry Street with the Englishman. Old Clothes was pushing his hand-cart in the same direction. Beside him walked his half-pint wife, nursing hacked shins and a purple eye, the only person really injured in the fray.

She looked at her mate. 'Ye med a right show of yourself anyways,' she said.

'Well, I'm a showman.' he argued, 'Am'nt I always been a showman. What ails ye?'

I looked at the Englishman. I would not swear to it, but I think he was beginning to catch on.

The Long and the Short of it

There is growing up in this city a dangerous prejudice against a valuable and, hitherto, peace-loving section of the community, which, if not checked, will ultimately lead on to massacre and civil strife. I refer to the campaign, sometimes open, sometimes insidious, against the long fellow *qua* long fellow.

At street fights, excavations, installations, evictions, fires, demolitions and all the other occasions that go to make up the social round, the long fellow is always to be seen on his own, shunned by the crowd. If he is not a member of the Garda, the crowd seems to imply that he has all the makings of one. If he is not an immigrant from Ballyvourney, it is because he comes from Kiltimagh. Either way he is bad news.

Not all Dubliners are dwarfs and I have known West Cork men who could not tip the six-foot mark, but this myth of relative footage is deep-rooted in the Dubliner's mind and it colours his whole attitude to the question of long fellows and short fellows. A man may roll his vowels in the depths of his adenoids or rattle every consonant against the uvula, but if he is over six feet in height he is still regarded as a black foreigner in his own home town.

I knew a man one time whose height was six feet seven inches and whose background was as Dublin as the Poddle river. In spite of his great height he was, most times, gentle as a lamb, and very necessarily so, because five feet of him was leg and the other nineteen inches body. This did not incline him to overready participation in arguments or street fights; he found it difficult enough to balance himself as he was.

One Sunday evening he got into a row in Summerhill just after the seven o'clock closing—a time alas when, due to the overhasty quaffing of pints in an effort to beat the clock, he tends to suffer from a temporarily inflated ego and a consequent attitude of non-circumspection in regard to his fellows. His opponent, a local of those parts, who went under the soubriquet of 'The Bullock' was a little barrel of a chap who came to five feet whatever way you measured him. My friend was wearing his Sunday suit, which is padded at the top and specially designed to conceal the fact that five feet of him is leg.

The crowd were unanimous in their interpretation of the affair. 'A humping big countryman trying to hit up The Bullock,' said the crowd. 'Lurry inta him, Bullock,' advocated the crowd. 'Use your head, Bullock.'

By the time the squad car arrived my friend had two ribs cracked from The Bullock's shrewd, close-in elbow punching, and his lower row of teeth were hanging out from the well-timed butting of his opponent's head. The squad promptly arrested him and charged him with an attempted assault on The Bullock; the crowd followed him up to Fitzgibbon Street Garda Station to lynch him; and at the end of it all the DJ gave him a suspensory sentence of six months, informed him that he was a coward and a bully to use his weight on a smaller man, and was going into the question of compensation for The Bullock's injuries until they discovered that The Bullock had no visible injuries worth compensating him for.

My friend, who weights about seven stone, now drinks nothing stronger than lemonade, and, to make assurance doubly sure, goes around all the time in a wheelchair.

The prejudice is even worse in sporting circles. Up in the Acres the shrimp is always the darling of the mob, 'the little dinger, always plays a blinder, he does.' And so he does, because, apart from being a Hindu sacred cow, there is no occupation under heaven more free from obstruction or impairment than being a four-foot soccer player in Dublin.

The situation has become particularly dangerous to long fellows now that the small man has achieved confidence and knowledge from watching Jimmy Cagney and Mickey Rooney. Time was when the only function of the small man was to be married to a large woman so that cartoonists could make jokes about him. Then came the Hollywood cult of the 'little tough guy' to show him that not alone could large women be knocked about with impunity but that large men, once he got them on the ground, were no bigger than himself.

What this town badly needs is a revival of confidence in the long fellow. We must not go round with crooked shoulders apologising for our existence; we want to shout it out loud. It's not as if we can't match them, hero for hero. If they have their Cagney, we have our Cooper; if they have their Cuchulainn we have our Jack Doyle; if they have their Maurice Walsh we have our

The old red-and-white barber's pole

Lennox Robinson; if they have Jimmy O'Dea we have Noel Purcell; and for their Sean T O'Kelly we have de Valera. The large man, we must point out, is a Gael; the small man is a Firbolg. Indeed it is questionable whether the small man is entitled to any civic rights at all, and debatable whether he should not be condemned outright as a form of un-Gaelic activity.

We must regard the small man much as they do in the Rugby Union where, on the rare occasions that they do get hold of a small man, they put him in at scrum-half and then deem it legitimate, and indeed in some quarters praiseworthy, to use him as a spare ball. Only by such methods can we hope to make the city safe for the long fellow again, and rid it for all time of the pestiferous cult of 'the little dinger'.

A Good Trim All Round

I have deserted my old-fashioned barber in his Capel Street shop and have fallen a prey to ultra-brite, ultra-modern hairdressers in an O'Connell Street saloon. My old barber got taken of a 'flu and, too much of a rugged individualist to permit a first sub to take over, closed his shop for the duration of his illness. For two weeks I awaited his return. Then, hounded by friends and family alike, I sidled timorously into an incandescent saloon. I went in looking like a superannuated sheep-dog. I came out looking like a candidate for Cruft's.

Now every time that I pass an old red-and-white barber's pole I avert my gaze in shame at my betrayal. My old barber held himself to be a mere artisan, and looked like a butcher stale from his slaughter-house. My new hairdresser deems himself an artiste, a tonsorial artiste, and looks like a surgeon fresh from his operating-table. The pleb in me regrets the honest slashing of the artisan; but the snob in me enjoys the delicate snip-snipping of the artiste, and I fear that I shall never return to the primeval simplicities of common barbering again.

My old barber had only one chair, a vast leather-and-mahogany throne that looked more suitable for electrocutions than for haircuts, and evoked shivery memories of Sweeney Todd. Yet it did give one a momentary feeling of social prominence, elevating one above the other customers as they discussed the news of the morning. So different from my new saloon, where a dozen victims can be simultaneously snipped.

There was also a sacrificial aspect to the old barber's chair, with the hairier customers soon reduced to the aspect of sacrificial sheep; and this sacrificial aspect was intensified by the presence of the sole assistant or 'boy', whose immemorial function it was to prepare the customer for the ministrations of the Maestro, and who brought to his function a dedicated and reverent air. Unfortunately the off-white sheet that he wrapped around the customer could never prevent the smaller hairs from working their way down the subject's spine, so that every haircut would have to be succeeded by a bath and a fresh shirt or the prospect of being prickly for the remainder of the day.

My tonsorial artiste would not tolerate such liberties from clipped hairs. He wraps up the neck in two gleaming white linen sheets and a napkin, and pads it so closely with cotton wool that not even the most errant hair can slip through. His stern eye and firm hands seem to give individual attention to each and every hair on the head; for days subsequently the things stay put, exactly as he left them. Sometimes I think he paralyses them, not merely with lotion, but with dread of him.

Getting a haircut from my old barber was like sitting down to a formal six-course dinner, and took almost as much time. There was the careful brushing and combing, the first scissors, the first MA-chine, the second scissors, the second MA-chine, and the final scissors with teeth in it to thin the stuff on top. No use assuring my old barber that Nature was already having a go in that direction; he never permitted more than one option, more than one deviation from his routine. 'Will I lave ye yer locks, sir?' he would tolerantly inquire.

My tonsorial artiste only takes five silent minutes for the job, and he took my locks in two contemptuous flickers of his hands, without as much as a by-your-leave. He knows how to go delicately with the dubious patches on top, where the hairs never seem to know whether they are coming or going. He never has to ask me to incline my head back or forward, his infallible knuckles incline it as it should go; his magic, dexterous hands swoop and swirl with never a pause. He has machines that go squirt, machines that go blow, machines that go suck, and machines that go whirr. But he leaves me with the feeling that somewhere along the line he has permitted himself to become a sort of honorary machine, and I imagine that if the electricity were ever to fail he would fail with it.

Then if my old barber's haircut was akin to a sacrifice, his shave was akin to a sacrament. The 'boy' always applied the lather, enveloping not alone the cheeks and the chin, but the mouth, nostrils and ears as well. Through the fungus of foam the Maestro would then appear, accompanying each fearful swipe of his cut-throat blade with a sentence from his epistle of the day:

'Ah ... yis,'—*swipe swipe*—'the stuff isn't the same at all today, no nor them that's pullin' it either. Belvedyar an' Clongowes,'—*swipe swipe*—'that's what ye have inside of the bar counters now, sure couldn't ye tell them be the cut a their collars. Twenty minutes of foosterin' it took wan young whipster to pull me a pint t'other day, an' do you know what he said at the end of his foosterin? "I only hope," sez he, "I only hope,'"—*swipe swipe*—"'that I'm after pullin' it outa the right pump" . . . Isn't that a tarrible reflection,'—*gash gash*—'on the edewcation they'r dishin' up in them places, hah?' and the foamy cream would turn a sympathetic red as my blood stained the lather.

My new artiste never gashes. But then my new artiste has no strong feelings about things. He does not worry about what the men in the Kremlin are thinking. He has no interest in what 'them shower of wasters over thar in City Hall' are doing to Dublin. He cares not whether the oul' Shels are at last due for a comeback, and he bears no hatred for them 'doirty' Rovers. The time of the artiste is his money, but my old artisan could annihilate time. His approach was as one with Orpen's famous porter at Westland Row, who used to reprove impatient passengers with his philosophy: 'Thar's many a wan is above thar in Mount Jerome or Glasanevin today, an' they not caring wan bit whether they catch a train or not.'

Then why not go back? you ask. Ah well; I was not five minutes out from my tonsorial artiste when I met an old friend. She looked at me as though she was seeing me for the first time. 'My goodness,' she said, 'is that you? Why you look YEARS younger.'

A man is only human; and even Samson fell for that one.

'Offeecials'

Whenever I consider the hatred and contempt with which officials are regarded in the world today, I shudder in gratitude to my people that they never tried to make me into one.

In every country the official has become bad news. In Latin America they assassinate him; in the US they investigate him; in the USSR they liquidate him. He is for ever being embroiled in financial or amorous scandals in France, while in Britain they serenade him each morning at breakfast with rapturous banner headlines like *Planners Humiliated Again by Residents of Little-Pudleigh-in-the-Vale*.

But these things are trivial compared to what the official has to suffer in Ireland. In Ireland the citizen does not content himself with a sporadic or accidental spleen against officials; he goes to bed with it at night and wakes up with it in the morning. The word has even acquired a special distinction in our national language (the unofficial one); it is the only word in the language that can be mispronounced in the same way by both the countryman and the Jackeen. 'Offeecial' says the countryman, of his county manager. 'Offeecial' says the Jack, of his clerk in the Labour. They both mean the same thing; and in neither case are they meant as compliments.

People defend this spleen by saying that it has to do with the seven centuries of oppression. This is a poor excuse. In the years of oppression the official was just a hired man, saying 'Sir' to the gentry, and sitting in a cubby-hole until required at the big table. The spleen goes deeper than that. The spleen lies in frustration, brought about by thwarted desires.

Every Irishman longs with all his soul to be an 'offeecial'. Where English boys dream of being engine-drivers, the Irish boy dreams of being a station-master. If he emigrates when he grows up, he can give free rein to his desires, and so the world is littered with the bones of Irish officials, from Tammany Hall to Mandalay. But at home he must curb his desires for fear of what the neighbours would say. His talents for officialdom rust in him unused. He develops a spleen; becomes a critic; and foams at the mouth every time he sees a uniform or gets a letter describing him as *A Chara*.

The most puzzling thing about this anti-official spleen is to try and figure out how it can be reconciled with the duty of Christian charity towards the human person.

The crowd that go to Lansdowne Road, for example, are a very civilized lot, given to the ideal of fair play, and not desirous of showing too much of the old Adam. Get there on the day of a Final Trial, with the Possibles beating the Probables, and you see something of their real nature.

Every time the Possibles score, there is a savage roar of exultation, and five thousand leering, sadistic eyes look up into the middle of the West Stand where the five selectors sit—five decent inoffensive men, whose only crime is that they have sacrificed a happy life for the good of Ireland. But to the crowd they are 'offeecials', and every time a Possibles' score proves them wrong is an occasion for another round of drinks on the way home.

'Quintet of stumers,' gloat the crowd. 'I wouldn't be in their shoes tonight if Ireland never won another match.' And the pity of it is this; there is not a man in that sadistic five thousand who is not quivering with the desire of being in their shoes, if only he had the chance.

The Gaels, too, have their spleen against officials. But they do not go in so much for their selectors; they keep it for the County Board. A man may be well-liked in his county until he gets elected as secretary or treasurer of his county board. Then he achieves a status he has never known before. His

Every Irishman longs with all his soul to be an 'offeecial'

ancestors are dug from their graves, his skeletons rooted from ancestral cupboards. His friends take up the monthly reports of the meetings in the local newspapers, trembling for the glorious news that he has run off with the funds. He never does, but they never lose confidence. 'That fellow,' they tell you, 'has bad blood in him and *it will come out in him yet.*'

Brooding on these things, and trying to reconcile these irreconcilables, I came one day to where the road to Clonskeagh leads to the Dodder river. In the distance, sounds of battle and strife gave evidence that the Rovers were playing the Shels at Glenmalure. I wandered up and stood beside a large man with a voice trained in battle by many a Liffeyside siren. Beside the man, his ten-year-old son was piping shrill epithets at the Rovers' full-backs.

'Now, son,' reproved the man, 'you mustn't be one-eyed. You must be fair to the other team.'

'Even when it's Rovers, daddy?' protested the amazed youth.

'Even the Rovers, son. Remember, Rovers is huming beings too.'

I saluted this most Christian gentleman, and had I been Archimedes I would have yelled 'Eureka'. The man returned my salute, suffusing himself in proud appreciation of his own two-eyed fair-minded nature.

A few minutes afterwards, a Shelbourne forward dribbled towards goal and was roughly but fairly tackled by a Rovers' full-back. The forward jumped

34

three feet in the air and rolled a further ten feet into the Rovers' penalty area. 'Peno, ref.' he called, more in hope than in confidence. The referee, to whom this gag was as corny as last year's cheese, waved on play.

From beside me came a deep volcanic rumble, followed by a series of half-strangled, supersonic bangs. Then . . . 'Ye baldy, half-witted, bloody oul' blinded-eyed bat, ye. Why don't ye take the hair outa yer eyes an' see what's goin' on . . .'

I gazed, stupified, at my two-eyed friend, while his face turned purple with the force of his rage. Then, even as I listened to the litany, I had the answer to the problem of Christian charity and the official in Ireland. There was no problem. There was no moral conflict to be reconciled.

OFFEECIALS . . . IS . . . NOT . . . HUMING . . . BEINGS.

Look out for the Ball-Man

Some folk refer to him loosely as a chancer; others pithily as a bum; most just call him a scrounger. But in those quarters where people are reared to have an exact word for everything he is known simply as the 'ball-man'. Of all the sharp citizen-types in this town, there is none more enigmatically elusive of analysis than he.

He is the great master of one of the time-honoured ancient crafts, and in the subtlety and originality of his methods he bears as much relation to the parasites of other towns as Michelangelo bears to men who carve turnips into effigies at street corners.

To be 'in on the ball', in the language of the commonalty, is to be in when things are going buckshee, and the ball-man gets his name from the fact that he never fails to be right on the ball. Committee rooms of cup-winning football teams on celebration night; opening nights of public houses in new suburbs; wakes, weddings, presentations, launchings and births—he has them all taped, and wherever things are on the house he will invariably be found in the house. If he does not know the man on the door he knows the hole in the wall; if there is a grant or a subsidy going he always qualifies; if there is a soft job in a new Coras he will never be caught looking for it—he will always be found sitting in it.

The ball-man, unlike the drone, is never shook for the readies; his desire to get things free arises from a congenital aversion to putting his hand in his own pocket. Like a sort of human cuckoo, he is cheerfully prepared to lay his eggs in anybody's nest and he gets away with it because citizens of this town, in common with birds, have never really learned how to catch the cuckoo. For us, the credit customer will always be a gentleman and the man who can only pay in cash little better than a tramp.

It is the mark of a true ball-man that he can live where a camel would die. The genuine article is born, not made, and although all growing boys are ball-men by natural instinct, and students are very often ball-men by temporary necessity, they are not really ball-men *per se*.

The ball-man *per se* can be distinguished from an early age, and his career is shaped to a consistent pattern. As a small child he will be found clinging to his own unwrapped piece of toffee while he happily shares that of his more unthinking friends. As a boy he will be found tampering with the back exits of cinemas; for while no self-respecting boy ever dreams of paying his sixpence until he has first tested the rear exit, on the off chance, the junior ball-man will not even consider bringing his sixpence with him.

When he grows to adolescence he deserts the back exits of cinemas for the front entrances to dance halls. He never tries to crash the barrier as a 'slag' would, nor does he promise assistance against other slags in return for his own free entry, as is the custom of the 'banner-man'. He just seeps his way through; if permitted to stand around long enough he is capable of seeping his way through a front door as oil seeps through a rag. To throw him out is futile. He will leave the hand as swiftly as a boomerang and like a boomerang he will return faithfully to the spot from whence he has been thrown. Between the Scylla of being lagged by the Law and the Charybdis of being done by the doorman, he steers a perfect course, in the true faith that everything comes to him who waits.

The ball-man may be said to graduate from the dance halls, but he practises in the pubs. In the pub there is no resisting him for by the time he reaches public house age he has learned all there is to know about his craft. There are ball-men who will ask you for their 'entrance money' (the price of one pint) and on the strength of it they can drink all day on the offerings of perfect strangers. There are ball-men so expert that they can attach themselves to any group and, no matter how you vary the tempo of the orders, it will always be closing-time just as their turn to buy comes. Nor will they hit their turn on the first, tentative 'Now GENTS' of the publican which is a mere implication that there is another ten minutes to go. They always hit it on the final 'NOW Gents', beyond which there is no appeal.

We will never get the ball-man out of this town. He has now become a social necessity. In the old days, when Dublin used to have professional boxing tournaments, you always knew the champ coming in by the number of ball-men in his entourage. It is the same today with tycoons and even Governments. A man who is well surrounded by ball-men can safely feel that he has arrived; it is as good as having old masters in the drawing-room or entries in the classics.

Then, again, it does need a certain collective instinct to get rid of the ball-man, and we do not seem to possess that instinct. I knew a soccer ground one time with a high but scalable wall bounding one of its sides. They used to keep stewards behind the wall, each one patrolling his own section, to keep out the chislers, slags and ball-men.

This particular afternoon one of the stewards was missing, and over his undefended piece of wall the chaps were clambering happily. A stout and irate citizen, on his way down to pay at the gate, stirred into civic spirit by the frustration ·engendered by his own· inability to climb walls, addressed protesting remarks to the nearest visible steward . . .

'Aye Mac. Are yez not gonna do somethin' about them ball-men going over yer wall?'

The steward looked indifferently down towards the action. 'That,' he said, 'is not my humpin' bit of wall.'

And that I suppose is why we will never get the ball-man out of this country.

A Lament for Old Nosey

They have banished Old Nosey to Ballyfermot. The emigrant cart (now become a familiar sound in our street, as rumbling a portent of execution to its inhabitants as ever the sound of the tumbril to revolutionary Paris) has carried him off, with his goods and his chattels and his uproarious long-tailed family, to his new home in the country. We do not know by what miracle of bureaucratic ingenuity they finally managed to extricate him from the brown bricks and the area railings, nor do we know what system of defence in depth they will devise to prevent his return. All we know is that we are much the lesser of his departure, and with his going life seems to have gone, too, out of the buildings.

Old Nosey was the happy extrovert of our company, a man for whom life went by on epic wings of great happenings. We used to look inwards; gloomily at our empty pockets, apprehensively at our bodies, pessimistically at our souls. Old Nosey never had time for introversion, sin or sickness. He was always looking out at the passing parade, or down into the mysteries of the earth, or even up to where the planets or the men from Mars would greet him with daily promise of sensation.

Nobody knew how old Nosey was. The grime of Dublin was creased and patterned in every crevice of his wrinkled face, and our local publican seemed to think that he must originally have come with the licence. For six days of the week he looked after the tangled threads of his long-tailed family, and then, on Friday nights, he would take leave of them, to discuss over a few pints the sensations he had gathered during the week . . .

'Did yez see thar whar 'twas gev out . . . on the wireless?' Thus, in a voice suffocating with the wonders of the world, Nosey would open his theme for the evening. He would sit on the highest stool where he could command the view, his nostrils twitching, his eyes jumping, a cross between an amiable ferret and a mad spring hare. Then he would proceed to develop his piece of news, and such was his magic that within five minutes the muttering, discreet, small groups would have coalesced around him into a wonderful debating society of speculations and surmises, where the only rule was that no member should know what he was talking about or, if he did, should have the manners to conceal the fact.

I do not know what the radio men and the publishers would do without Nosey. On him half the fortunes of Fleet Street must have been founded. For him were invented the flying saucers and the Digests, and he must surely have invented Question Time on his own account. Yet he is not a demanding reader, and in quiet times editors do not even have to invent a silly season for him. Every season is Old Nosey's silly season, and he could, if put to it, extract as much sensation from a Central Bank report as a lesser man would get from an earthquake.

His two great vices were the Sunday papers and the Law Courts. 'I seen thar, whar 'twas gev out . . . on the Sunday papers.' He would buy, not one or two of them, but every one of them, right down the list, and his Sunday would then pass in a flashing progression of 'follier uppers', every one of which was taped and memorized for future reference.

The Law Courts were to him what football matches are to the average man, and the only time we ever knew him to knock off from work was when some case in Green Street or the Four Courts proved too strong an attraction. Yet, in spite of his fascination with the Law, he could never quite figure out what the cases were all about, and I always remember the Friday night he returned, puzzled and grave, from 'follien up' a famous and much-loved poet plaintiff in a libel action, to inquire earnestly, 'D'yez tink, lads, d'yez tink will he get a stretch?'

'I seen thar, whar 'twas gev out . . . on the Sunday papers'

Nor was it any use trying to reassure him that plaintiffs do not necessarily have to get a 'stretch' because they lose their actions. In Nosey's vision of the Law there were only two ways of coming out of it, winning or 'stretched', and even there again we were never quite sure that he had not the right of it.

Now that he is gone we try to speculate what new wonders he will discover in Ballyfermot. How will he miss the long summer evenings sitting on tenement steps, listening to the oul' wans screaming their news from window to window, or the sudden uproar and scuffle on the bank holiday nights and the hurried run down the street to see who was 'after getting done'? He will have many years, at any rate, to get used to his new suburb, for the Noseys of this world are generally far too busy looking at life to be unduly troubled by the fear of having to leave it. Perhaps in due course of years, after several abortive attempts to return to his old home, he will come to terms with his new environment. Then his infallible voice will be heard echoing over the river path at regatta times. 'Yer man thar . . . best boat on the river . . . been follien 'em up for months . . . it's always been gev out about them in the papers . . .'

One sees him going on . . . and on . . . and on, year following year following year, until some day, in a pub yet unbuilt, in a suburb yet unplanned, he will turn up his ear to a faint distant sound, and, first as always with the news, announce to the bar, 'Yez'd better hurry up with them pints, lads. It's just after been gev out thar . . . on the trumpet . . .'

Good Oul' Baldy

I sometimes wonder if those Sunday newspaper people who are always lamenting the decline of sport in these islands ever heard of Baldy. I do know that Baldy never seems to have heard of them. He cares nothing about international prospects or cup-ties, and news from the West Indies leaves him cold. The only thing, in fact, that he knows about games is that they are for playing, and he plays them.

I first met Baldy up in the Fifteen Acres, out on a windy, no-man's-land of sport, where numerous, small, muddy pitches encroach on each other and stretch away to the horizon. He was playing on the wing in a hurling match, a small man with a bare patch on his skull, and neat agile legs which did not quite seem to belong to his corpulent little body.

All around him flaked the ragged legions of back-pitch sport, their faded togs flapping around untrained, inexpert limbs. Baldy alone was creased and pressed and laundered, just as he used to be many years before, when they were small boys and he was playing at Croke Park, and having his picture in the papers, and being asked for his opinion about things.

Now he was back to where he had started, not participating much in the wild slogging of the young fellows, but waiting for the loose balls, and then showing them, with the cultured stroke that had graced many a famous field, how it should be done. From the touch-lines the retired colleagues of his younger days looked on with committee-like disdain for his conceit, and deep secret envy of his spirit.

I began to follow him after that, and learned to look out for him on other back pitches. I would see him locking the scrums of minor-league rugby matches, exhorting the same keen youngsters, and demonstrating—when his wind permitted—with an occasional, perfectly controlled dribble. Then I would find him distributing the ball with calm, judicious passes on some underprivileged slobland of a soccer pitch. The circumference of his middle varied a bit from pitch to pitch, the bare part of his skull seemed greater or less from sport to sport; but I knew it was the same person, the joke and envy of his friends, and I knew they could never exclude him with age limits nor ban him with foreign games rules.

For you can only ban a body, and Baldy, as I began to discover, was not a body but a spirit, an antic spirit that flits around in the air and takes possession of certain bodies, forbidding them to age with their sinews, denying them the comfort of the pipe, the committee and the judicial air, urging them on with the one law—whenever you see a ball, kick it.

People call him by various names. Rude fellows in soccer refer to him as 'Head the Ball', but for all that they respect him. They respect him with a certain awe, for he is twenty years later than anybody else.

When his compeers are retiring to the golf course, he is still holding a straight bat at the wicket. When they go to the bowling green, he is thinking of playing golf. When they go to the deck-chair, he is wondering if he might play bowls to fill in the vacant time from playing golf. When everybody else is dead, it occurs to him that he might like a few years on the committee in addition to his other activities. But he is never the Grand Old Man of anything, because he never permits himself the luxury of age.

Age cannot wither Baldy, nor can even wives dissuade him from his course. Only once in all his many sporting careers have I ever seen him put down, and even then, phoenix-like, he was to rise from the ashes.

It was in a match in Fairview Park where a team of large, hairy men were playing a team of smaller, paler men. There was a most unusual number of oul' wans present, and getting beside one of those little bird-like citizens who always seem to know everything, I learned that the thing was a family affair, a dockside 'needler' between the Checkers and the Dockers. The Dockers were four goals in the lead, and my-font-of-information added by way of explanation, 'the Checkers is nairvous.'

I could see his point. Apart from having to give away considerable weight, they were also faced, at centre-half for the Dockers, by a well-known sporting

The missus of a sportsman

character of the neighbourhood, whose custom it was to clear his lines, in the manner of Bould Thady Quill of Muskerry, by braining anybody who dared cross them, and so the Checkers forwards had obviously resigned themselves to a blank but safe afternoon.

Then, stung by the 'nairvous' display of his forwards, Baldy began to move up from half-back, where he had been quietly playing for the Checkers and amiably receiving the advice of the oul' wans to go home and bring his missus to the pictures.

Suddenly there was a long, despairing kick from a Checkers' full-back, an open space, a singular reluctance on the part of the Checkers' forwards to move into it, and there was Baldy, racing the big centre-half for the ball. He got there just before his opponent, placed the ball neatly in the Dockers' net, and collapsed under fourteen stone of dock muscle.

It was 'good oul' Baldy' now, and the oul' wans gathered round, supporting the stricken figure of Baldy's wife. Even through her lamentations,

I thought I detected a faint air of triumph, an incipient 'I told you so' that, at long last, with three ribs broken he would finally have to retire and admit her in the right.

But, poor vain woman, she will be telling him so for many years yet to come, for only last week I saw him back again, playing for the lowest, muddiest team in the business, the only team that he could persuade to accept him, but still playing. For there is only one end to Baldy, and it applies to all Baldys everywhere, from masters of foxhounds to masters of slobland soccer. When Baldys die, they die with their boots on.

The Guv'nor, the Sir, and the Baaws

The old-timer had obviously been shocked to his soul . . . 'A pair a young aye-literates thar in the packin' department this mornin',' he explained. 'Thar they were, singin' at their work, an' the Guv'nor standing oney a few yards away. SINGING: An' the pewer man havin' to stand thar lissenin' to them. Well I went down an' I lit on the whipsters.

"Would yez mind," says I, "to cut out that singin' and larn to show a bit a respec' for the Guv'nor."

"For the WHAT?" says the pair of aye-literates.

"For the Guv'nor," says I.

They looked at me with their iggerant mouths hangin' open like they might have thought I wus somethin' brung down outa some strange planet.

"The Guv'nor," says they. "WHA'S THAT?"'

A sad story to be sure; the conventions of a lifetime outraged by an unholy generation that knows not the Guv'nor. But who does know the Guv'nor today except his dwindling remnant of faithful old-timers? We aye-literates can only guess about Guv'nors. Solid men, one imagines; dignified, ponderous, patriarchal; stiff wing-collar, stiff neck under it, stiff upper lip above it; respected and dependable as the pound sterling of their day.

Consider, however, before you condemn us aye-literates, the history of the case. Once every firm had its Guv'nor. The Guv'nor knew everybody and everybody knew the Guv'nor. But when I came into business it was already the age of the 'Sirs', the men who knew all about the 'science' of management; who never dealt in workers, but went in exclusively for 'personnel'. The Guv'nor died either with the bang of '14 or the whimper of the twenties. And now the Sir is also going, dying more sure than any Guv'nor.

It was the rise of the big Corporations that killed the Guv'nor, but it is the Planned State that will do for the Sir. In the Planned State Jack no longer needs to be as good as his master, because his master is no longer a person, only an abstract, and the Jacks are no longer even personnel, only man-hours.

The Guv'nor was tough, overbearing at some times, and a court of no-appeal at all times. But he was personal, intimate, and when he bawled you out he bawled you by your first name. The Sir was more impersonal, remote. But he was at least a physical presence, something that Youth could envy, not like the modern Coras which is beyond envy, beyond spleen. No Jack wants to be as good as his Coras.

So Youth gave up using titles, and the ex-Sirs called Youth names. 'Insolent!' said the ex-Sirs: 'Disrespectful!' 'Irreverent!'

Foolish ex-Sirs; not realising that Youth, even in this teddy-boy age, requires its hierarchic order as much as it needs its food. Youth was busy looking for a new symbol of authority. And what I asked myself, as I watched them come, earn their first exciting week's wages and disappear in a few months to the flesh-pots of Birmingham, would this new symbol be?

Last month I got my answer. It arrived in the shape of a sixteen-year-old citizen, a candidate for a job left vacant by a departed émigré. Even as junior citizens attire themselves these days, he was pretty colourful. The shirt was technicolour, draped around the neck with a piece of purple material that was not exactly a flowing bow-tie and not exactly a length of rope tied up in knots. The jacket, which reached almost to his knees, was a rainbow tweed with a velvet collar and broad shoulders that looked as though they had been stiffened and padded with planks of timber. Under it he wore a satin waistcoat of black and white check. You could have played chess on it.

I sent him off to clean a plate-glass window from the top of a ladder, and then, overcome by curiosity as to the Beau Brummel waistcoat, I went out to discover the origin of the species.

'What do you call that?' I indicated the garment.

He looked down at the waistcoat with pride. 'That, baaws, that's a Mississippi Waistcoat.'

'Does it come,' I asked in all innocence, 'from Mississippi?'

'Naw, baaws,' he said patronisingly, 'It's called a Mississippi Waistcoat because Rock Hudson wore it in his picture *The Mississippi Gambler*. All the chaps is goin' in for it now, baaws . . . .'

So there I was, and there you are, my good ex-Sirs. Of what avail our Institutes of Management, our benevolent bayings from our we-up-here-and-you-down-there platforms? These cockerels want a 'baaws', just like the old-timer wanted his Guv'nor—a personal Mississippi-Waistcoated baaws who

The last attack

will bawl people out by their first names, just like the old Guv'nor used to do. Next Monday they will be in for 'the loan of a few bar till Friday, baaws', because their wages will have been spent to meet their Mississippi Waistcoat instalments on Saturday.

And what shall we do to meet the challenge? Do we let our shirts get darker, our ties get brighter? Where shall we find the cackle of a Widmark, the muscles of a Marciano, the drive of a Cagney, the nasal menace of a Bogart. The Sir is dead, from his hand-tailored gent's suitings to his hand-made shoes and his conservative gent's shirtings. Forget him. Look West, middle-aged man, if you want to be baaws today.

For 'baaws' is coming your way, too; if me today, you tomorrow. I see this thing spreading from my small frontier outpost down Henry Street to O'Connell Street, capturing draperies, groceries, pharmacies, solicitors' offices, pubs, warehouses. I see it infiltrating Parliament Street for a flank attack on Dame Street through the soft underbelly of the insurance companies; overwhelming the stiffer defences of Anglesea Street and the Stock Exchange; marshalling its troops in College Green for the last attack on the final fortress, where, behind the classic pediments, the Ionic and Corinthian columns, the stout granite walls of the Bank of Ireland, the last of the Guv'nors sits surrounded by the last of the Sirs.

A BAS LE GUV'NOR . . . VIVE LE BAAWS.

The Perfect Wife

Sometimes, sitting around in pubs, ear wigging on discussions, I hear citizens arguing (usually when they have exhausted every other topic) about what particular quality they would most prefer to have in a wife. Some say humour; others say tolerance; others call for efficiency. I never say anything, for though once, some years back in the forties, I did encounter the perfect wife, I have never been able to find a name for the quality that made her so.

In those days I used to frequent a pub back of the Ormond Markets, where musically-minded citizens of the quarter used to hold a singing party every Saturday night. No messing or communal harmonies or sing-as-you-go chorus work, but strictly one-man-one-voice stuff, with a neutral MC elected to see fair play between the singing men. Since I was the only regular who was not related by blood or marriage to somebody else, I finally made the post of MC my own.

It was a post of honour, but not relaxing. There was the necessity to be ever vigilant against the various messers, bawlers and brawlers who get attracted to singing houses as do moths to flames. Still, in spite of the ebullient tendencies of the Dubliner when being wooed with concord of sweet sounds, we managed to get along without either broken glass or broken noses.

The regular singing men, chief of whom was a large and ferocious bankman from the Markets, who rejoiced in the incongruous sobriquet of 'Queenie', were tough citizens, very jealous of the singing privilege allowed to them by their liberal host, and anybody who looked like messing up the pitch on them was usually given a swift exit. As time went on we began to develop quite a name in Dublin musical pub circles, with virtuosi coming from all over town to try their talent against the locals.

And then, one Saturday night, came Jumbo.

I did not need the frantic warnings of Queenie and his committee to inform me that here was bad news. One sight of the eager moon-face, one sound of the stentorian tones ordering the pint, was enough.

Poor Jumbo was that most tragic of artistes, a man with the soul-quality of a Caruso and the sound-quality of a thousand jackdaws, a man doomed to wander from singing-house to singing-house, with every MC's hand against him and never a stage to call his own.

As the night wore on, however, Jumbo's face began to hypnotise me. Every time I looked around to call the next performer the face would be there before me, the face of an impatient, excited dog, waiting for the ball to be thrown his way. I could not resist it. It made me feel like a monster, keeping water from a man dying of thirst. Finally I gave in, and, to the outraged glares of Queenie and the committee, I called on Jumbo. He rose with alacrity, sang a dirge fifteen verses long, and sang every verse in a voice like a bucket-dredger at work in the bay.

I went into the night with my reputation in shreds. 'Yew,' reproached Queenie, 'that's supposed to be a man of mewsic. Yew, that claims to know what's what. Well, if ye want to go on being the MC around hyar, son, ye better make up yer mind to blow out that head case next Satturday . . .'

There was no help for it. I had to blow out Jumbo the following Saturday, trying not to be aware, as the evening wore on and whistler followed singer, and yodeller followed reciter, of the lineaments of the large moon-face opposite me, changing from expectancy to doubt, from doubt to disappointment, from disappointment to resignation. It was obvious that the experience of being frozen out of the performers' list was no new one for Jumbo.

But he kept on coming back, and bore no ill-will. If he could not sing for us, he was prepared to listen. Indeed, as a listener Jumbo was first-division stuff; his enthusiasm and the generosity of his applause were as good as five pints to any man's vocal cords.

Then, one Saturday night, he came accompanied by a spry but fragile little creature, whom, after he had carefully placed in a corner behind a bottle of cider, he introduced as 'Maro—the Missus . . . just outa the hospidil after a job done on her stummick,' he added, for while not being one of those utterly reactionary types whose proud boast it is that 'I never took out me oul' bird but wanst, an' that wus the day I took her down to the Pro to get marrit to her,' Jumbo was enough of a Dubliner of the forties to know that an

A large and ferocious bankman from the Markets

explanation is due from any man seen out with his own wife on a Dublin Saturday night.

Maro enjoyed herself immensely, sipping her cider with the perky movements of a sparrow, and growing brighter in the eye with every song and every sip of cider. The songs rolled on towards the curfew hour, and now we were reaching the stage where the leading men, the founder-members of the Society, were privileged to take the floor. I looked across at the hard Queenie to see if he had reached his proper form. He rose with becoming dignity, and made his way with due and proper gravity to the piano.

Even as he reached the pianist, Maro spoke.

'Mister,' she leaned over graciously like a queen about to confer an unexpected honour, 'Jumbo hyar is a sin-ger too.'

There was a scandalised shushing sound from Jumbo, outraged at his wife's breach of Proper Order. But Maro's eyes were now sparkling as brightly as the cider in front of her.

'Jumbo is a luvely sin-ger,' she announced to the scandalised assembly. 'Go on Jumbo; show the people!'

A deadly hush fell upon the pub, while we waited for all the fish, fruit and vegetable market buildings of the quarter to fall down around us. And, even as we sat there frozen, Jumbo rose. The temptation was too much for him. He took one huge gollop of his beer, made his way to the piano, turned his earnest mask to the ceiling, and began to howl. The veins of his neck pulsed and swelled as he lavished over us all the pent-up frustrations of his silent nights. He had low notes like ships' sirens; he had high notes like locomotive whistles; he had top notes like the brake-linings of CIE buses. And all the time Maro sat listening to the awful cacophony with a rapt delight shining on her face, as though the dulcet pipes of Pan were calling her from some remembered groves in Arcady.

Jumbo gathered himself for his final, pealing ululation:

'Oooooy knaow,' he wailed, 'we both would doooy;
Moooy heaAAAAAAART and oy-hoy-hoy.'

There was a silence. I looked at Queenie, the man who knew what's what. A tough man was Queenie, the winner of a thousand Dublin brawls. But, though he well knew how to burst an enemy, he had never learned the more subtle craft of how to hurt a feeling.

'Maro,' said Queenie, 'that was luvely . . . that was the best we've had . . . that . . .' and you could see him tearing the words up from the unwilling roots, 'that deserves a-a-a-an awncore.'

Maro turned to Jumbo. 'Go on,' she said, 'show the people.'

Jumbo went on. For all I know, he is still going.

The Pint

The Same Again, Sir?

Defendent, in evidence, said that one of his regular customers had held a share in a sweepstake ticket that drew the winner of the Cambridgeshire, and was celebrating his win, in the traditional Dublin manner, by buying for the house. His difficulties in clearing the house, the defendent went on, were increased by the fact that there seemed to be an unusual number of unfamiliar faces present.

... NOW PLEASE LADIES AND GENTS NOW PLEASE MISTER BURREN THEY'VE ALL HAD ENOUGH NOW MISTER BURREN NO MORE ORDERS NOW MISTER BURREN I SAID TAKE DOWN THEM GLASSES CHARLIE ...

... C'mawn in lads quick; c'mawn, the gargle's goin' buckshee; will yez hurry on thar Budger before they get the door closed again ... Ah! Thar y'are Mister Burren; the rare oul' Mister Burren; wan a the best is Mister Burren, definely wan white man; yes Mister Burren we'll have the same again sir ... Order! Order thar for a vote a thanks from oul' Budger here ... will yez go aisy; will yez give the man a chancet to get a sup in him first ...

... An' is it Mister B. hisself the hard oul' sojer Mister B. d'ye·remember me at all? That's right mister B. an' thank you very much I'll just have wan little large wan Mister B ... Well here's to the good oul' sojerin' days Mister B. wan a the oul' brigade is Mister B. as dacant an' bitter an Irishman as ever done his bit for the oul' country. I'm telling ya Mister B. Them was the days, hah! No sweepstake draws in them days, hah! Ye jes drew it in Portabella first an' if ye were fast enough offa the mark ye drew it a second time in Beggar's Bush, hah! hah! hah! ...

NOW MISTER BURREN PLEASE NOW LADIES AND GENTLEMEN CHARLIE I SAID KEEP THAT DOOR CLOSED LET 'EM OUT THE SIDE WAY NOW LADIES WILL YEZ SET A GOOD EXAMPLE THAR ...

... But reely Jewla, reely now wouldn't she make you sick the way she's always talkin' about him an' boastin' about him being an' office manager ... Well granted Jewyla, granted they are spendin' it dacent but whew wouldn't

Mister B. hissëlf the hard oul' sojer Mister B.

Jewyla, I mean what less would ANYWAN do . . . I knaow Jewelya, but reely, sittin' down here all night long talkin' about his oul' jokes an' how smart an' witty he is, reely to lissen to her ye'd tink he hàd a tooken the ticket outa the drum hisself, sure the man isn't even threatened with intelligence . . . Now reely Jewelya, do yew reely tink that oul' Burren could hold a candle to poor oul' Cassidy at home even if the poor man is destroyed with the ulsters . . . Now thar Jewyla, *thar is a reely witty man* . . . wait'll I tell ya what he said to me the other night Jewelya . . .

51

. . . NOW LADIES WILL YEZ FINISH UP THEM DRINKS PLEASE HAVE YOUS NO HOMES TO GO HOME TO HAVE YEZ NO FAMILIES TO MIND NO OFFENCE MEANT NOW LADIES BUT WILL YEZ TRY TO SET A GOOD EXAMPLE PLEASE . . .

. . . Lissen John; don't be took in by that oul' crook Burren I can tell yew that's the most ondeservin' man that ever won anything. Lissen thar I was last week, Skinnier was after ringin' up wid a hot wan for the four o'clock at Kempton and me without a tosser. So I hang on for the oul' crook to slip outa the office at half three for his usual thinkin' I might have a ging at the petty cash y'knaow . . . oh just a loaned y'knaow . . . oh that's wan ting about me I don't believe in that knockin' off game that game is bad news . . . Well anyways . . . THANKS VERY MUCH MISTER BURREN WE'EL JUST HAVE TEW PINT BOTTLES BE THE NECK UP HERE MISTER BURREN BEST A REGARDS TEW YEZ MISTER BURREN . . . Anyways, I makes a beeline for the box the minit he goes out an' as true as I'm sittin' here John d'ye know what the oul' bags has left in it? . . . Fifteen I Owe Yewez: *Fifteen I Owe Yewez*, an' it only the second day a the week an' thar the bleedin' oul' nag skates up in the four o'clock an' me widout a tosser on it an' thar's that oul' crook goes an' wins the bleedin' sweep YOUR GOOD HEALTH NOW MISTER BURREN AN' THE HEALTH A THE MISSUS . . .

. . . No but reely Jewelya, you've no idea the things that man Cassidy can tink up. Another night . . . wait, I must tell ya this wan . . . another night he cem home loaded to the gills an' I started givin' out ta him not that I reely minded Jewyla but I was always nairvous of the oul' ulsters wid him. Well Jewyla; quick as a flash he turned on me, an' out in front of the chislers an' everythin' . . . 'Good oul' Queenie,' sez he, 'Good oul' Queenie; when ye die I'll have ye stuffed an' hung up on the end a me bed to remind me of ye.' Now reely Jewyla, reely do yew tink that oul' Burren up thar could tink up a compaliment as good as that' . . .

. . . NOW GENTS NOW GENTS IT'S GONE FIFTEEN MINUTES OF THE TIME NOW GENTS WILL YEZ FINISH OFF THEM GLASSES WILL YEZ SHOW A LITTLE BIT OF CONSIDERATION CHARLIE I SAID PUT THE BOLT ON THAT DOOR . . .

. . . Order! Order now for a few short words of appreciation of Mister Burren's generosity from his oul' mate oul' Budger hyar; c'mawn Budger get up thar an' say yer few words . . .

. . . No! No! No! Never mind them fellas an' their stewpid talk. No, I mean let's take a serious queskin a histry now . . . I mean, take yew as an American . . . I mean do yew as an American deny that we Irish MED America . . . Yes

Give the man a chancet to get a sup in him first

but I mean take ANYWAN in American histry now, take Custer now . . . I knaow; I knaow he wasn't but if he wasn't wan hisself his grandfather was . . . well all right what was Custer's regiment'. . . sairtindly at Little Big Horn . . . well I'll tell YEW; the fightin' Sixty-Ninth, that's what they was, the Irish Brigade . . . Amn't I tellin' yew . . . Didn't they always march to the tune of Garryowen . . . Well whar did they get it from if they wasn't Irish? . . . From d'English? . . . WHA? HEW told yew that . . . 'Xactly; ye read it in a bewk . . . An' WHAR might I ask, was that bewk published? . . . 'Xactly: An' do yew as an intelligent man, I mean I presume that y'are an intelligent man, do yew think that that crowd over thar in England is goin' to give us any credit in a bewk . . . my dear man, did ye never hear of the paper waaaal? . . .

. . . Hould him back thar . . . hould back the impident bowsie . . . G'wan ye ongrateful pup Budger, comin' in here to drink Mr. Burren's beer an' then bringin' up old scores . . . Don't mind him Mister B. sure we all know your record Mister B . . .

. . . NOW GENTS NOW GENTS WILL YE TAKE IT EASY I'M SURPRISED AT YOU MISTER BURREN GIVING YOUR HEED TO A GURRIER LIKE THAT BUDGER FELLA I SAID NO MORE DRINKS CHARLIE . . . WELL ALL RIGHT SO MISTER BURREN SEEING THAT 'TIS YOURSELF IS ASKING . . . NOT THAT BOTTLE CHARLIE . . .

The Justice, imposing a heavy fine, said he would like to remind defendant that there were some traditions that could be more honoured in their breach than in their observance (laughter). If, he went on, the defendant Byrne was now in a happy position of being able to endorse a cheque, he would remind both defendants that he, the Justice, was in the happier position of being able to endorse a licence (renewed laughter) . . .

Culture

C'mawn the Chap

Some people ask: 'Where do chislers go in the wintertime?' I never have to ask . . . I know. They go to the children's cinema matinees; and until a man has tried to run a children's cinema matinee on a wet week-end in winter he has not really encountered the true meaning of the word ferment.

Officially there is no such thing as a children's cinema matinee. They become children's matinees at week-ends only because nobody else, barring a few tough oul' wans or a few deaf old-timers, would go next or near them. The chisler pays sixpence for his admission. For his sixpence he deems himself entitled not alone to see the picture, but also to burn the roof over your head and swipe the floor boards from under your feet.

From the transaction the Government gets a penny, while the cinema gets the fivepence and the chisler. It seemed like a good proposition when they first agreed to it, but basing costings on just what a chisler is able to do to a cinema in the course of a two-hour show, it is now realised that it would have been more profitable for the cinema to have taken the penny for itself and left the fivepence and the chisler to the Government.

One's first aim in running a cinema matinee should be to form your customers into a queue. This is a pious hope. Chislers, with their deadly perception of frail human nature, know that the more awkward they make things for you the harder you will work to get them in out of your way. For this reason they do not wait patiently in line. They come hard at you out of the queue, ten abreast, not dealing in convenient silver currencies, but in sticky collections of pennies, halfpennies, French francs, buttons, medals and bits of lollipop.

While you deal with these men of property milling around the cash-box, you must also be prepared to deal with the men of straw milling around the vestibule . . . 'Aye Mister, do I have ta pay for this young wan she's only a babby . . . Mister, me tanner is after goin' down a hole in me pocket . . . Mister, I was in an' I only went out to buy apples . . . Mister, me brudder is after runnin' off wid me tanner . . . Mister, the mammy says will ya give us

Chislers in wintertime

the tickets now an' she'el be down after . . .'

Having finally got the chislers into their seats the next object should be to keep them there. The children's seats are known as 'woodeners'. They are long running benches of deal wood and cast-iron and began life in the days of William S. Hart when furniture was meant to have a future. Each chisler is by law entitled to a foot and a half of woodener. The great advantage of the woodener is that it is hygienic, unbreakable, unstealable, uneatable and incombustible. Chislers cannot get knotted up in a woodener; they can hack it, stand on it, or jump up and down on it without damage to either the chisler or the woodener. For these reasons, while cinerama may come and cinemascope may go, the woodener will go on as long as there are chislers.

The selection of a programme for the customers is the easiest part of the job. A chap on a white horse. A pal on a black horse (to put the pal on a white horse would be tantamount to shaking hands with the butler). A villain on a stolen horse. A love interest for the oul' wans. Mix them all together in a story as old as the Trojan horse and you cannot go wrong.

For the rest, the customers can enliven any sentimental interludes for themselves with mouth-organs to augment the celestial choirs, catapults to break the pilot lamps, *Hotspurs*, *Wizards* and *Rovers* to read during the love scene, butts of apples to throw at the heroine, known contemptuously as 'The Wan'. Sound rises from them in great waves, while a ruthless operator forces the amplifiers until the walls shake and the chap's tenderest whisper of love becomes an asthmatic roar. All for action are the chislers, boys and girls alike, living with the chap, dying with the villain . . . 'Hit Him Up! Hit Him Up! Hit Him Up! C'mawn, C'mawn the Chap!'

A chisler, for matinee purposes, remains a chisler until he or she reaches the age of fourteen. The knotty problem comes when one is forced to confer, or rather enforce, adult status. Girls will decide the problem for themselves, changing overnight from lanky, tangle-haired slatterns to poised young beauties with high coiffeurs and higher heels, coming in like young duchesses on a slumming tour. Boys, on the contrary, will fight to remain boys to the bitter end, though pimples, cat-whiskers and voices like frogs' croaks give them the lie. But gamely they try: 'Mister I'm only thirteen . . . the brudder will tell ya . . . I'm only thirteen . . .'

There is nothing harder under heaven to deal with than a rogue boy at a cinema matinee. He has so much to hold on to that his smooth ejection requires a technique of surpassing delicacy. Place one arm affectionately round his shoulders, concealing from any adjacent oul' wans the fact that you have the half-nelson on him with the other. If he is a game rogue, he will manage to hack your shins on the way out in a ratio of one hack to every three steps, but at all costs keep on looking like a good, kind man, beaming down on him, and beaming genially on the oul' wans as though everybody is the best of pals. When you get him out the thing can develop into a fair race between your foot and his rear-end.

If with any luck (and you DO need luck) you land one on him and he brings back his oul' wan, do not argue the point. Let him in again, and when she is safely back with her oven raising her cake you can be safely back dealing with him. The only thing to remember, at chislers' parties, games or matinees, is this: 'There is no such thing as a bad boy.' Not as long as his oul' wan is around to argue the differ, there isn't.

The Light of Other Days

I wonder where the hard men of the music hall go for their entertainment today, in this fashionable, pre-London winter of their discontent.

What started me wondering was the sight of the old-timer who had wandered innocently into the Olympia and into the first night of a play obviously destined for the West End. It was far from the boiled shirts, up at the top of things in the gallery bar. Round the bar a polished preen of young intellectuals had gathered for the interval. Pretty young women were sipping cider. Long hairs were waving fluctuating hands over amber glasses of beer. Sterner men in duffle-coats were brooding darkly into bottles of stout, thinking deep thoughts.

The old-timer stood transfixed in the doorway, gazing in mingled apprehension and rage at the youthful usurpers of his throne room, while the scars of a hundred battles throbbed in sympathy across his pummelled face and over his great broken buttress of a nose.

'When did this happen?' he asked.

I eased him gently to a far corner of the bar. 'Did you not know?' I asked in surprise.

'Amn't I beyant in Glasgow these years,' he roared, 'and no wan to drop me the word what's goin' on. PLAYS!' he bellowed, 'PLAYS in Dan Lowry's!'

He had come, I gathered, like a pilgrim returning to a shrine, dreaming of theatres that wore pink tights and orchestras that had trombones in them. He had found in their place, as he put it, 'a collection of talking merchants, without a decent act in the lot of them'.

And yet, like a true Dubliner . . . 'It's not the few bob entrance I mind,' said he, 'only for the thrupence I'm after droppin' for the programme.'

'I seen the day,' he commented morosely to the bottle of stout that I offered him, 'when a man that ordered a bottle of stout in this bar would be lifted out of it . . . ladies not served, you'd be told.'

Apologetically I indicated back of the counter, from whence all traces of the famous pumps of other days had been untimely ripped and only the bottled stout was in evidence.

He gazed. 'True as I'm standin',' he breathed, 'are they after doin' away with the draught porter? Amn't I able to get a proper pint for drinkin'?'

I shook my head and watched him shrinking before me. Thus I thought must Oisín have shrunk before St. Patrick, or Rip Van Winkle on his return from the land of sleep.

'I suppose,' he said softly, 'I must be comin' to this oul' gods since the day I earned me first tosser. I drank me porter here in the twenties when there was more madmen standin' round this bar that you'd fit into the 'Gorman, roaring out their oul' stories of the Marne and the Somme and bawling *The Long Way to Tipperary*. I seen a squealer thrun from the back of this oul' gods with nothing between him and the nobs in the circle but the oul' wans hanging outa him. I seen the northside boys come over the river wan night and we bet them out of it and down the alley and through the Dolphin. The diners could have drunk Monto blood for soup that night . . . we spilt so much of it.'

He stopped to gaze in sudden amazement at two pale youths who were drinking pale sherries in the corner. Around them, under the spell of his reminiscences, I seemed to see the shades of his fabulous and vanished company; the old fusiliers, the swift shadowy men of Monto, the solid battling men of the Coombe, the lusty river men of Irishtown, and the great muscular dockers from the island parishes. Now it was the day of their Diaspora, and I wondered by what strange waters they were mourning for their spangled Zion.

It could not be films. That stuff might do for their sleek, two-dimensional sons with the crew haircuts and the Edwardian jackets. But what is the shade of Betty Grable to one who has known the reality of Dorothy Ward? Who cares for Betty Hutton when he has cheered for Gertie Gitana? How can even the greatest 'talking merchants' of their legitimate age be compensation to a man who has learned theatre from the Chocolate Coloured Coon? There is nothing left for him now but to sit in the pub, and tell sad stories of the death of stars to an audience that heeds him not.

A sudden bustle interrupted my reverie. The crowd were moving out for the

second act. The old-timer shook himself. He took a long, last look, like a king about to go into exile.

'I think I'll mosey down to the oul' Queens,' he said 'I might still be in time for the second house . . .'

I let him go, without telling him. Let him find out for himself, I thought, and if he drops another threepence for a programme, I do not want to be around.

Exhibitionmanship

Consider, says I to myself, this question of Culture for The Common Man, the plain blunt son of a spuds-and-bacon clan who yet may be anxious for to shine in some aesthetic line.

He looks around him for some simple Gilbertian line, such as sitting on the daisies and discoursing in novel phrases of his complicated state of mind. And he finds it's no go for complications any more. Dublin culture has become all hard graft and specialisation. Work up your culture-gimmick and stick to it; that's the rule.

Now the trouble about culture-gimmicks, at least for men like myself and yourself, not overburdened with either the brains or the readies, is that all the best ones have become either too cheap or too expensive. Bookmanship has been vitiated by the cheap, paper-backed editions of the classics, travelmanship been tainted by the cheap, coach-backed editions of the classical Grand Tours. Wininganddiningmanship has gone to the other extreme; there is not a single, cheap, porter-backed edition of a classical Joe Skinner to be got today in the city of Dublin.

What then, you ask, is the working man to do? Must one go back to booing referees and breeding greyhounds again? No! There is a better way: EXHIBITIONMANSHIP: the finest manship of them all. With very little time, and practically no thought, you, too, can become an exhibitionman.

Exhibitionmanship—i.e. the systematic attendance at all exhibitions arty, crafty, trendy, cultural and practical, is not alone a lovely culture for to have, but it is also a nice dry way of spending wet afternoons. It gets you into the way of gentle exercise in amiable surroundings, and it gets you into the way of meeting the best people in town, or passing through town; Lords, Dukes, Earls, Film-Stars and TV Panellists are to be found literally littered all over the exhibition halls. Moreover, once you acquire the knack of avoiding the eye of the lady who sells the programmes, you get the whole thing for free.

What are the prospects for the right kind of young man? Very good! There is quite a plethora of exhibitions on the Dublin scene these days, but a scarcity of good exhibitionmen. Modern exhibitions tend to leave the average chap groping for words. Faced with a hall full of things that could be jugs, horses, teapots or chairs, average men—indeed quite unaverage men, Godotmen, Bertholt Brechtmen and FinnegansWakemen—go into reverse. Their minds boggle; their tongues twist; their hands, normally so mobile, pause petrified in mid-air.

Now there is no necessity for such panic. A good exhibitionman does not necessarily have to *know* about the things being exhibited. Properly equipped, a good exhibitionman should be able to handle anything from Henry Moore to an antique dealers' fair. The equipment: A bow-tie, for accentuating whatever intellectual lines one has on one's face; a strong but sophisticated umbrella for leaning on and pointing at; and, most important of all, a pair of rubber-soled shoes.

One cannot emphasise too strongly the necessity of rubber-soled shoes as an item in the equipment of the exhibitionman. Many exhibitions are held in small halls or galleries, where the floors have neither rugs nor carpets, and where every footfall sounds like gunshot. There is nothing that marks the novice more than the ignorant, loutish clatter of leather-soled shoes across the parquet floor of a hushed, exclusive little gallery. Such an entry compares most unfavourably with the stealthy, confident pad-padding of the experienced, rubber-soled exhibitionman.

Having acquired the proper equipment, be content to begin in a small way, trying to remain as inconspicuous as possible during your early training period. Attend only exhibitions where the hall is so crowded that nobody notices you (e.g. the RHA on the opening day of its annual); or exhibitions where the hall is so empty that there is nobody there to notice you (e.g. the RHA on any other day of its annual).

After some time you will learn to differentiate between the five major divisions of people who are to be found at exhibitions.

1. Those who go to be seen at them.
2. Those who go to see who else is at them.
3. Those who go to see what's at them.
4. Those who go to write about what's at them.
5. Those who go to buy what's at them.

Of these groups the first three can safely be ignored; the last two are the form horses to follow (if you can find them). If they sniff, sniff. If they frown, frown. If they purse the lips or shake the head, do you likewise.

Do not, however, under any circumstances, attempt to handle exhibits at this stage. A most promising young exhibitionman of my acquaintance had his whole career ruined by knocking over a mysterious piece of ceramic at a recent exhibition of Italian glass and pottery in Grafton Street. The thing did not actually break, but my friend never recovered from the shock of the noise it made; and the scornful looks he got from all the superior-looking types around him who had not knocked over anything will live with him to his dying day.

On the question of when the novice exhibitionman should first begin to express himself in actual words there are various opinions. Myself, I favour a probationary silent period of at least six months. Exhibition language is full of pitfalls; and there is simply no use in having all the right gestures if you are going to ruin the effect by having all the wrong words.

For this probationary period, the student should content himself with grunts, vague choking sounds, or deep sighs. Avoid expressions such as 'aaaayxquisite', 'luvely', 'raaawvishing', 'sorta kinda like y'knaow', or 'Aunt Minnie has wan jus' like it at home in the parlour.'

Be careful also with jargon. You can acquire jargon easily enough, but the ready use of it comes trippingly only to those people who go to sleep and get up with whatever things are being exhibited. It is bad to splutter in any language, but to splutter in jargon is the social end.

After you reach the stage of being able to formulate meaningful, ongoing, relevant, viable words without making a fool of yourself, the next step is to develop independence of judgment. By this stage you should have had experience enough of modern exhibitions to be able to hazard a guess at what most modern exhibits are supposed to be.

Confidence is now very essential. Only a few weeks ago I entered a hall to find everybody crowding and foostering around an enigmatic-looking apparatus supported on long, slender legs that tapered off into near invisibility at ground level. They poked the thing apprehensively; they fingered it uncertainly; they frowned over it and hovered around it and knelt under it. I took one quick look at the yoke, and, even while they muttered and argued around me, I knew I had it taped.

I SAT on it; it was a chair.

The final stage in the course of the young exhibitionman comes when he has acquired the necessary poise, confidence and gabble to be able to demand (and get) every time he enters an exhibition, the immediate attention of the promoter, curator or whatever power may for the moment be. The capture of the promoter is the crowning glory of exhibitionmanship. When you capture the promoter you automatically form a procession, and, as everybody in the hall cannot fail to observe, *you* are at the head of the procession.

This is the moment that will repay you for the months of silent, cringing anonymity, for the hard, early weeks of blush-making gaffes.

This is *EXHIBITIONMANSHIP.*

On Spreading Sunday Culture

I remember the time I first started going in for Sunday Culture, way way back before it had begun to spread all over the town, and sometimes I wonder if I am maybe in some way responsible for the spread of it.

It was not long after the war, I remember, and I had been invited by mistake to an intellectual party where most everybody else present was a promising young something-or-other. I was trying hard to get off my mark with a soulful-looking young woman of great beauty against the opposition of a superior person called Harold Something, whose principal social weapon was his uncanny ability to make everybody else feel inadequate to whatever social occasion happened to be in it.

Harold was giving out about some chap called Hindemith . . . 'Such Vigour! Power!! PUNCH!!!!' enthused Harold.

The soulful one turned her doe-eyes on me 'What do *you* think?' she breathed.

'Why I-I-I- don't rightly know,' I stuttered . . . 'I don't think I ever saw the guy fight.'

There fell a dreadful silence over the room, and then everybody started moving away from me and eyeing me askance and muttering things about me. Afterwards a friend explained to me how Hindemith was a celebrated composer and how I was a thick.

I knew then that I would have to start going in for the Higher Things if ever I were to get off my mark with talented and soulful-looking young women, and shortly afterwards I discovered those two Sunday journals which for many years subsequently were to be my guides in all matters of high-thinking and loud-talking around Dublin.

It was a convenient time to discover them. Paper rationing was still in force and culture had to be compressed within eight or ten pages. I remember (with tears) how I used to 'do' one of the journals while waiting for the pubs to open at one-thirty and finish off the other during the five to seven period, the second session as it was known.

Then, in addition to being compressed, the culture journals were also very scarce at that time, and only those sharp off their Sunday-morning mark could get one at all. At that time, however, I was manager of a cinema much beloved of juvenile newsboys north of the Liffey, and, next to Alfie Byrne ranked Public Figure Number One in the eyes of northside chislers. So it turned out that, whoever else went short of Sunday culture, I always got mine.

This gave me a great advantage over most other Sunday-culture people, because it meant that I was good for at least one Authoritative Opinion on every subject, and indeed two contrary Authoritative Opinions on most subjects, while other folk were lucky to have an Authoritative Opinion about anything. At such intellectual parties as I managed to crash you could hear me giving out all over the room on Art, Music, Current Theatre, Whither Europe, and Trends In The City. It got so that finally everybody else went back to moving away from me and eyeing me askance and muttering things about me.

That, of course, was in another decade, and how was I to know that finally I would get so caught up with Art, Music and Whither Europe that ultimately I could no more forego my Sunday culture than I could forego my Sunday pint? But while my Sunday pint consumption remained more or less constant, my Sunday culture consumption seemed to expand and expand.

I don't know for sure when matters started getting ahead of me. These things sort of creep up on you rather than hit you suddenly. But Sunday by Sunday the course seemed to be getting that little bit longer. It would not have been so bad had I been one of those shrewd selective readers who go straight to what they want. But I was an all or nothing reader, who felt guilty unless he had read everything. I was accustomed to going it all the way from World News on Page 1 to Sport on Page 10; and as Sports began its slow march back to Page 12 . . . 14 . . . 18 . . . 20 . . . 24 . . . 26 . . . 28 . . . 32 . . . 34 . . . my Sunday reading began to spread over Monday, Tuesday, Wednesday, Thursday, Friday, Saturday . . . I began to develop an ulcer and a harried look, and once again people started eyeing me askance.

They say that if a man lifts a tiny bonham new-born, and goes on hoisting it faithfully day by day as it grows, he will still be able to lift it, without effort, when it has become a great, fat, meaty pig. It may be so with pigs; it is not so with culture.

One Sunday my intellectual back broke under the weight. *The Observer* contained 34 pages; *The Sunday Times* ran to 36. A kind of hopeless feeling came over me. It seemed as though somebody over there in Fleet Street was intent on making of me a bloated repository for all the high-thinking in the world. I tottered into the nearest pub with my head spinning.

I left about an hour afterwards, physically refreshed but still mentally numb. I had not even got as far as Ffieffer, which will show you how bad I was. Then as I walked down the street I felt an unaccustomed lightness about my normally heavily-laden Sunday-morning person. I reached for my jacket pocket. My *Observer* was no longer in it. I must have left it in the pub.

I turned to go back for it, and then stopped. Suddenly I got all come over with a wonderful idea. I knew that I could never desert the Higher Things after all those years . . . *but I could LOSE them* . . .

All I had to do was to walk into a pub, read what was of most importance to me, and then, carefully leaving my journal on the counter, make a swift dive for the door before my conscience could start getting at me or any interfering busybody inform me that I was forgetting my paper.

So I have been doing ever since. It is just like the old happy post-war days again. I read my *Observer* for the first session. Then I lose it. I read my *Times* for the second session. Then I lose it, too. I pick a different pub every Sunday so that nobody can get wise to me. And I congratulate myself that it is a far, far better thing for Culture that I do now than I have ever done . . .

For think of all the cultured grocers' curates there are going to be around this town before I finish getting around all the pubs.

Götterdämmerung

Were you ever suddenly landed in the middle of the great unknown; empty of knowledge, full of questions, strayed accidentally out of your native fish-and-chips top-twenty culture into a new strange scene, nothing much between the ears, one and threepence and six Woodbines in the pockets?

Picture me thus—how many years ago?—staring in wonder at a long line of people that stretched from the half-light of South King Street to the dusk of Mercer Street.

Carmen, a man said. I knew nothing of it and cared less; but when you don't know the score the queue is a powerful magnet. So for a shilling—or was it ninepence?—I followed the tumultuous legion of the queue's rearguard, up stone steps and around breathless corners, to a landing that welcomed us without benefit of linoleum or carpet.

In front of me were backs and shoulders. Above me a ceiling bellied six inches from my head. Below me a gallery sloped—no; hung suspended by the

grace of God—as it creaked and groaned with the weight of bodies close-packed upon it.

I fondled my threepence and thought sadly of my lost shilling. Then, deep deep down in the depths of some other soft plushy world, a man in white tie and tails appeared, raised his hands over an invisible orchestra, and from the vasty deep sound crashed and soared like magic:

> *TAN ta ra ra ra ra ra: TAN ta ra ra ra ra ra;*
> *TAN ta ra ra ra ra ra rahahahahahahah;*
> *TAN ta ra ra ra ra ra: TAN ta ra ra ra ra ra;*
> *TAN ta ra ran ta ra rahahahahahahah . . .*

went the magnificent musicianers; and so, my back-bone disconnected from my hip-bone, my neck-bone disconnected from my back-bone, and half a dozen latecomers connected like limpets to my head-bone, I first heard the opera *Carmen* from the late Gaiety gods.

What a gods! How does one even begin to describe the scene to one who has never experienced it. To sit at the back and look down its precipitous slopes was a test of a man's nerve; to sit at the front and feel the massed weight of the tiers of bodies rising sheer above you was a test of a man's heart. It defied the laws of gravity, and it scorned the demands of law, order, polite society and equilibrium.

There were uniformed attendants who were not your servants but rather your hosts; who cheerfully discussed last night's performance with you while the curtain was down, and determinedly fought you from their sacred gangways and steps when the curtain went up. It had gentlemen singers who entertained you with arias during the intervals. It had regulars so ancient that you wondered how they had ever made it up all those labyrinthine steps. It had a bearded resident tramp who, on less crowded nights, used to lie full length in the back row snoring his way through the performance. It was unique among gods . . .

I went up the other day to visit the grave. I looked up to see, where once hung the soaring shrine of all our yesterdays, an upper circle so gently tiered that it would not have disgraced a super-cinema. Suddenly a great despair for all the coming generations of young opera-goers, the lost souls who would now never learn their opera through the medium of sore bones and an ache for every aria, fell over me.

For surely these sacred high places in the theatre were meant to be the domains of Youth and of Age, of the student and the pensioner, and of nobody in between. And is it not a terrible thing to see the high places being usurped today by upper circles, 'from all parts of which you are guaranteed an uninterrupted view of the stage'? Are not the backs of young fellows strong, the necks of young ones supple? Was it not to overcome the interruptions that they were so fashioned in the first place? And are not the memories of old folk faithful? What need have they of any view? They have seen it all before.

Up there now every customer will be guaranteed his own personal private seat, and—by the sacred boards and woodeners to which we once clung—every seat is going to be a cushioner. *Cushioners!* Where generations have sat upon each other's shoulders and stamped upon each other's heads.

I do not know how you can expect to rear enthusiasts from soft seats. The soft seat and the uninterrupted view is the philosophy of education that rears the drop-out; for Youth, when it no longer has to fight for its view of things, loses interest and turns to a looking-glass to view its own discontented reflection. The long wait on a cold queue is the best apéritif that a young fellow could have, and the hard bench in a high gods is a good heady wine.

The seat of the intellect is in the dress circle, but the promenade of the emotions needs a spacious gallery in which to express itself. But a circle of cushioners puts a careful limit on rapture. How do you roar or boo or whistle or scream in a circle, and to stamp your feet on a carpet is just about as rewarding as to try and slam a swing door.

It is a great shame that niggard law and modern usage no longer approve of gods, for a theatre without gods is like a body without blood. The gods is particularly the heart of the opera house, even if its pulsing life has always been kept at a snobbish remove from the body to which it pumps life. We give it the poorest entrance, but it retains the richest spirit. We treat it like the poor relation, and all the time it is the grand-da.

We cannot replace a gods with an upper circle. We leave to the artist the same wide lonely world before him as he rings up the curtain; but we have stripped the broad thundering heaven from above him, and the loss is both his and our own. So weep then, Pagliacci, for a love that has ended . . .

The Passing of the Chap

The intellectuals are infiltrating. First the Empire; then the Queen's; now 'The Ranch'. Today, over a sound-system once sacred to the Texas drawl, can be heard the liquid Latin of Lollobrigida. On seats once sacred to the devotees of the sombrero and the six-gun can be seen a sprawl of duffle-coated dudes and sophisticated squatters.

What'n tarnation? To think that 'The Ranch' should have died, not because of a lack of customers for its goods, but because of a lack of goods for its customers. For its death is part of a pattern—the decline and fall of the 'chap'; and it marks the final scattering of the men of the west.

Where are they now, the old familiar faces? Hopalong is touring the world. Gene and Roy, Silver and Trigger, are riding the television range. Buck Jones and Tom Mix have crossed the great divide. Tex Ritter, that tuneful troubadour, ready at the very cock of an enemy's gun to burst forth not alone into action but into song, has become a mere singing voice on the sound-track of another man's High Noon. Charley Starret (beloved of the younger chislers for the manner in which he could take six men at one go, but suspect of the older chislers as a 'shaper') is gone back into civvies; and Wild Bill Elliot is gone tame. Is it any wonder that my old customer, Bang-Bang, connoisseur of the Western cult and chief impresario of the Western way, comes to the pictures no longer?

So what, I hear you say, there are Westerns still, on wide screens and in colour. But goldarn it! These are not the real McCoy; they are mere vehicles for men like Cooper and Stewart—shapers who could turn up next month like as not as bespectacled boffins.

The true Western chap was never guilty of such inconsistencies. He was invariably and reliably faithful to his own particular story, style and sombrero. And the true Western was classical in the strictest sense, confined within its rigid convention of plot (chap rides over the hill—chap rides back over the hill), dialogue (yeh gosh-darned young whipper-snappers yeh), time (sixty minutes dead) and locale (the same scrawny patch of Californian scrub, with a rock for the chap to jump from and a half-mile level straight for the chap to rescue the wan from off the bolting horse).

This was the product known to the trade magazines as 'routine thick-ear, good for juveniles, adolescents and unsophisticated audiences'. But if you look back at them (now that you no longer have to actually look *at* them) you will see that they had in them much of the stuff that went into the epic tales of chivalry, even if the lutes were replaced by guitars and the damsels were too handy with lariats to be easy prey for dragons.

For Hopalong and Gene, like Roland and Lancelot, always rode out without expectation of reward. For them, it was simply the thing to do. And when the battle was over they always rode back again into lonely Western sunsets, strumming softly on guitars and *alone*. Not for Gene and Hopalong the slippers and the fire and the Happy Ever After.

It was the same with their prototypes in city dress, those slick perennials of the asphalt jungle, *The Saint* and *The Falcon*. A bit more worldly-wise with the

The lonely sunset

damsels perhaps but Harry Whartons at heart. They had no lonely Western sunsets to ride into but they invariably took cabs back to lonely bachelor flats, ready to turn up next week free and unencumbered by the ordinary chores of life.

Were these things, then, the answer to the unsophisticate's need of plain tales, or were they an answer to the adolescent's need of an ideal that would be at once both heroic and untouchable? Now that I come to think of it, was not that how I used to fall in love at the age of fifteen, demanding of the loved one nothing more than that she should get mixed up with a dragon so that I could rescue and, having rescued, ride off into a sunset that one never seems to experience after adolescence?

Thus the inviolability, the utter aloneness of the old-fashioned chap might have been something more than a mere convenience to keep him on the active list of chaps. Corny, no doubt, but for fifteen-year-olds corn is surely better than cheesecake, a foodstuff which can very quickly leave boys incapable of seeing the dragons for the curves.

Of course, the chislers are finding their own chaps, too, in this modern age. I met a seven-year-old customer of long standing in Parnell Street the other day. He hailed me, as is the custom of my customers, to inquire what was on the menu for the following Sunday afternoon. By chance we had a revival of one of the old-type Westerns coming up. I told him so, expecting to hear his pleasure at the prospect.

'Gaaar,' said the connoisseur, 'that ole stuff.'

Baffled, I glared at him! 'Well, what do you want?' I asked.

He looked away into some happy vision of his own, while his eyes grew round with the excitement of a memory:

'Mummys in graves, Mister,' he gloated, 'a-a-a-a-a-an green, sloimy tings comin' up outa the say . . .'

For whisper it gently; it is not the seven-year-olds who are mourning Hopalong today—it is the seventy-year-olds. The juveniles have their new age and the chaps in that new age are 'Its', 'Thems', 'Creatures', and 'green sloimy tings comin' up outa the say . . .'

The Pint

A Song with your Pint

One of the few rules of social etiquette whereon the average Dubliner and his guests tend to differ is in regard to the vexed question of whether or not a gentleman should be permitted, in a licensed premises, to sing with his beer. It is a matter of no little importance and leads not infrequently to extremely awkward International Incidents.

Picture, if you will be so kind, the following situation, a situation all too embarrassingly familiar to anybody at all familiar with the customs of Dublin licensed premises.

There, sitting on a high stool, is a friendly, broad-vowelled Glasgow-Belongs-Tae-Me tenor from Loughwinnock or Kirkintolloch; or maybe a decent Ilkla-Moor-Baat-At baritone from Yorkshire; or perchance a booming Blaydon-Races basso from faraway Northumberland of the Geordies. He and his mates have been enjoying themselves all evening in hospitable Dublin company and now, as the curfew hour approaches and the sentiment begins to flow as freely as the beer, he suddenly gets come all over with the notion of returning his hosts' efforts to amuse him by entertaining them with a little bit of a song. What could be more appropriate, he thinks to himself, than to sing them an Irish song, the only Irish song, more than likely, that he knows?

He lets back his shoulders, takes in air, stretches his arms around his mates' shoulders, partly for their moral support and partly to include them in the tribute. And then, a ringing northern voice proclaims to the house its firm, passionate, unalterable opinion that When Irish Eyes Are Smiling They Would Steal Your Heart Away.

What happens?

A pair of outraged Irish eyes glares from behind the counter. An Irish voice like the sound of a ton of gravel falling through a grating thunders:

'CUT OUT THAT SINGING.'

Meanwhile, all around the immediate neighbourhood, one can behold pop-eyed Irish eyes, apprehensive Irish eyes, indignant Irish eyes, and Irish eyes wondering if their Irish ears have deceived them. But there will be no smiling

Irish eyes, and the stranger's heart will be in no danger of being stolen away.

For in Dublin city (and this does *not* apply in Irish country pubs to anything like the same extent), a pub is either a singing-house with a special lounge entirely given over to music, or else a strict non-singing house where the first threat of a note being held aloft will send the landlord rushing headlong for The Law.

There is nothing in between. Discreet close harmony in a corner, falsetto keening to one's immediate company, *sotto-voce* warbling to oneself, or even a humming serenade to one's pint will all be deemed equally heinous. The Law demands that a singing-house shall manifest itself plainly as such. To make music without such manifestation is to make music without the sanction of your host, and therefore without the sanction of the Law.

There are, of course, a few exceptions to this rule, and visitors might like to note them down:

1. If you are a member of a wedding party that has been celebrating all afternoon in the same pub, or if you can attach yourself to such a party (by no means a difficult feat).

2. If you are in town celebrating Christmas Eve (but not—in most pubs—for some strange reason, on New Year's Eve.)

3. If you are a Welshman in Dublin in the week preceding or the week following a Welsh–Irish rugby international.

4. If you are an emigrant just returned from the land of the stranger.

In any of these cases there is no law against your singing in a Dublin pub. At least if there is, no means has yet been devised of enforcing it. Other than on such privileged occasions, however, it will be necessary for visiting public house virtuosi to go in search of that infrequent but honoured institution, the Dublin singing-house.

These, as I say, are not numerous. Many local citizens do not like music in pubs because it interferes with their favourite occupation which is talking. Others oppose it because it obtrudes on the weighty meditations with which they like to accompany their drinking. Still others resent it because they consider playing darts an infinitely more rewarding occupation. Publicans are nervous of it because it tends—with a certain kind of customer—to lead to unharmonious rival quartets and, ultimately, to belligerent attitudes and broken bones all round.

But when you do find a well-run Dublin singing-house, then you are in for a night's entertainment that will leave your Munich beer cellar or your Blackpool tavern way behind. For unlike these roof-raising establishments, where singing can be all too frequently a matter of uninhibited chorus work from all corners, Dublin singing-houses (in Dublin you never speak of a 'pub';

you always refer to the place as a 'house') are designed for solo singers only, and are run on the classic principle of One Song One Voice. You are reminded of this fact at frequent intervals by an MC who speaks in tones of sounding brass and the motto of whose refrain is 'ONE VOICE NOW LADIES AND GENTLEMEN PLEASE.'

This is known as Proper Order and is the foundation on which all singing-house society is based. It stands between the harmonious civilization of true singing men, and the cacophonous horde of howlers, bawlers, messers, hooters, moaners and flat-voiced bleaters who constantly threaten at the gates.

Without Proper Order the barbarians would ultimately take over and, therefore, the penalties for breaches of Proper Order in a singing-house are very severe, ranging from a public telling off at the voice of the MC to the supreme retribution of having your drink taken down, your money refunded, and your person escorted from the premises.

What, then, is Proper Order? How is it maintained and how does one offend against it?

Proper Order in a singing-house is primarily the concern of the MC who has to depend entirely on his voice and personality. Customers come under the requirements of Proper Order from the moment the MC mounts his platform (if he has a platform) and the pianist sits to the piano.

The master of ceremonies will open proceedings with the command: 'ORDER NOW PLEASE.' As of this moment a decorous and seemly hush should fall upon the house. The voice of a good singing-house MC can be heard over the combined noises of two hundred customers talking simultaneously, fifty customers shouting orders at ten waiters, and ten waiters relaying the orders to five barmen. Some houses employ another functionary known as the 'bouncer' to ensure a seemly hush, but in the élite places the 'bouncer' is only visible in extreme breaches of Proper Order.

It is an offence against Proper Order to enter a premises in a noisy fashion. If an artiste is in the middle of his performance when one enters one should remain by the door until he has finished his number.

It is against Proper Order to join in a chorus without the express (and very rare) permission of the MC. It is an offence to sing with or against the performer, or to orchestrate his melody by stamping one's feet upon the floor or banging one's glass against the table.

It is against Proper Order to start arguments about the rival merits of the performers if there is a competition in progress. (In some houses competitions themselves are against Proper Order).

It is an offence to be loud-mouthed, exhibitionist, or strident.

It is a heinous crime against Proper Order to offer oneself as a performer without the invitation of the MC.

Finally, it is a deadly sin against Proper Order to adopt a 'deroghetary' attitude to the performance of any artiste. No matter how awful a performer may be, he is still entitled to his performer's rights of due appreciation from the house.

There are three degrees of 'Order' as called by most MC's.

'ORDER NOW PLEASE.' This call is normally used to start the concert on its way. It is also used to introduce the early performers; reliable old ice-breakers; regular performers of no particular merit; or tolerated bores of no merit at all but who happen to be good customers.

'BEST OF ORDER NOW PLEASE.' This signifies the approach of some reasonably talented person; some local big-wig whose social position demands that he be treated on the same level as talent; or some particularly good friend of the house. Visitors, until they prove themselves otherwise, are always given the courtesy of this call.

'PARTICULAR GOOD ORDER NOW EVERYBODY PLEASE.' or 'THE VERY BEST OF ORDER NOW PLEASE LADIES AND GENTLE-MEN.' Either of these (the choice varies according to the social position of the house or the MC) can be regarded as the supreme panegyric, bestowed on the very few, and signifying that the performer (1) has arrived at the top, (2) has been there for a long and honourable period, (3) is confidently expected to get there.

Next to Proper Order, the most important feature of a singing-house for a guest to know about is 'The Form' of the house. 'What's The Form like up there?' is the first question a native would ask about a house to which he had never been.

The Form includes everything from the standard of the performing talent to the quality of the drink served to the kind of songs favoured by the customers. The Form is a much more elusive and varied thing than Proper Order; and The Form of a small neighbourhood house will naturally differ from that of a big singing-lounge.

If it be your ambition to attend a singing-house, not merely as a listener but also as a potential performer, then you should spend your first few evenings discreetly in the background studying The Form. All singing-houses, though this applies more so to the small intimate places, have their regular customers whose feelings have to be considered, and who would be gravely put out by the sudden appearance in their midst of a gentleman who could go right through *Largo Al Factotum* without a stutter, or hit a high C without strangling himself.

Hitting a high C without strangling himself

If you are a performer of this class then you should break it upon the house by slow and tactful stages so that you can be put back for your call to the final stages of the evening. It is terribly bad form for a singer of this class to allow himself to be thrown early into the proceedings, as it means that he will have put the skids under anyone who comes after him. (The point is not likely to arise, however, as singers of this class never do allow anybody to come after them.)

Singers of less shattering talent do not have to worry about this but they should still spend a night or two in the background before offering themselves for performance.

Offering oneself for performance is an art in itself, since one simply cannot just walk in and say, 'I'm a rare singer, d'yez want to hear me?' It is best done by first making friends with some regular customer and then, in the course of conversation, permitting the information to be dragged out of one that—'Well, now that you mention it, as a matter of interest, one does do an odd bit of singing oneself and, while not being at all up to the class of the house, well, one might be prevailed upon . . . in an emergency.'

Your friend will then inform the MC and, in due course, you will be placed upon the list of those to be called. In singing-houses not everybody is called, and indeed many have to be rigorously excluded.

When called one should approach the platform (if it is a really classy house it will have a platform complete with piano and microphone) and, with no false modesty or coy hesitations, inform the pianist of your intentions. You do not need sheet music—a good singing-house pianist can accompany any man on any song in any key. Indeed, sometimes, he has to accompany through a whole variety of keys.

Make clear at the beginning whether you are a comic singer or a serious singer, because in singing-houses it is not always possible to tell otherwise. And never take an encore without the permission of the MC. An encore means that you are knocking some other poor fellow out of his big moment. So be a good chap and hop down as smart as you hopped up.

You will find that The Form, as far as musical items go, is pretty varied. Modern pop-singers alternate with cheerful oul' wans and old-timers doing Gertie Gitana or Chocolate Coloured Coon routines. There will always be somebody (more likely some two or three bodies) to give a throbbing rendition of *Sweet Adeline*. Duets, Trios and Quartets are permitted *on the platform*.

You will be tolerated for a monologue; admired for a Tauber-type love song of Your Heart and You. Songs native Irish or Tin-Pan-Alley Irish will be received according to the mood of the house. Songs about caravans in the desert—*Where caravans have rested—Pitching lonely caravans at night*—are legit. Roses, from Picardy or elsewhere, are permis. Anything from *Maritana* or *The Bo Girl* will get you in the Best of Order class (but you had better be good at it because that stuff is as Dublin as cockles and mussels and we know to the nearest demi-semi-quaver of a grace note how it should be done).

But if you really want to go over big, you should sing a song about Mammy. Coal Black Mammy, Dixie Mammy, Old Irish Mother, Mother in The Highlands or Mother in the Lowlands—you just can't whack a Mammy song for a Dublin audience. Please do not ask me why this should be so. I don't know.

The most popular times for singing-houses are Friday and Saturday nights and what is known as the 'the second session' on Sundays (in summertime from four to ten p.m.). To be sure of entry to the most popular houses on busy nights one should present oneself before eight o'clock. The entrance to the singing-house may be full when you get there, but that does not necessarily mean that it is full inside. A gentleman is nearly always in attendance at the entrances of the bigger houses, not the least part of whose function it is to decide who is worthy of admission, and who is not.

Regretfully one has to warn connoisseurs of the national drink that the noble thing is not served in its pint tumblers in some houses. The pressure on space in many singing-houses is too heavy to leave room for pint glasses on small tables. Pintmen should, therefore, make a point of stocking up in the tap-room below before they go up to the smaller world of the half-pint glasses above in the lounge. Most landlords will accommodate you by reserving a place for you *as long as you are having your pints on their premises.*

The recognised centre for singing-houses in Dublin is the Wexford Street-Camden Street strip on the south side of the city. Behind this thoroughfare, bounded on the south by the South Circular Road and on the west by the winding length of Donore Avenue and Marrowbone Lane, lie the neighbourhoods of Belleville, Tenterfields, Pimlico, The Coombe, and the areas devoted to Sts. Patrick, Nicholas and Werburgh. As Trastavere is to Rome, as the Marais is to Paris, so is this quarter to Dublin. Here you meet the purest native types, hear the lazy Dublin accent with its authentic drawl unadulterated by vowel or consonant from the provinces. There are families living in these parts whose roots in the neighbourhood go back way beyond Dean Swift, and old-timers for whom anything north of Portmarnock, south of Bray, or west of the low road to Lucan is 'abroad'.

These are some of the people, with a fair sprinkling of 'foreigners' from north of the Liffey, who frequent the Wexford Street singing-houses. Here you will encounter Proper Order in its most formal manifestation. The full regalia is laid out; piano, pianist, platform, MC, microphone (for those who need it).

But while Wexford Street is the recognised centre for the Muse, there are other places where a man may sing with his liquor. In places north of the river along Parnell Square, North King Street or in the St. Michan's area back of the Ormond markets, musical evenings tend to be more informal. There is a famous house in Dun Laoghaire with a lively local crowd and a talented blind accompanist who plays on piano and accordion, while a few miles out, in Glencullen under the shade of the Dublin mountains, is a 'local house' where you can hear the best of old Irish ballads and where some of the regulars compose their own ballads.

There are smaller intimate little houses, too, like the one on the Quays near the Metal Bridge attached to a famous 'pint pub' where the folk of the quarter come for an informal sociable evening without such additions as piano or MC. Further up the river, through an archway and into an ancient courtyard, Dublin's oldest and most historic inn boasts a piano in the corner and permits of music by anybody who has a mind to entertain the house.

But please: northside or southside, city or suburb, big house or little house, the cardinal rule is: 'ONE VOICE NOW LADIES AND GENTLEMEN PLEASE.'

Places

The Waiting Hour

How exquisite it is, that tranquil Dublin Sabbath moment when suddenly, into the pitter-patter of leather soles on concrete, the susurration of rubber wheels on asphalt, there intrudes at about 12.50 p.m., a silence, followed by a short pause, as though somebody, somewhere, had just blown a whistle for half-time.

Now all the streets a Sabbath stillness hold. The last churchgoer turns his last corner home and leaves the town to tourists and to me. Benevolently we gaze along deserted pavements. Approvingly we note the most seemly hush that has fallen on all things. Soul-stirred, we conjure up visions of domestic peace behind red-brick facades.

It is the very resting hour of day, the hour for all good men to be coming to the aid of the digestion with armchair meditations, deep-breathing exercises, and anticipatory sniffing of the tantalising kitchen sniffs.

Or is it? Not by a deep quaff. Not by a dozen deep quaffs. Maybe for the natives of the thirsty thirty-one counties it is; but not for Mother Ireland's favourite drinking son, not for little metropolitan Jacky-boy. Before he may anticipate, much less partake of, his Sunday Joe Skinner, there is a certain formality to be observed. And, be it said for him, he observes it.

So, after a five-minute interval of empty silence, the streets and squares begin to fill again. First in ones, then in tens, then in hundreds, the sanctioned citizens of the metropolitan area reappear, white-collared, Sabbath-shaven, every man protected from cold by Sunday overcoat, every man protected from boredom by Sunday newspaper, every man looking, most justly, like a husband who has just quarrelled with a wife. They take up stations; they stand; they wait . . .

For what? For the thunderous, clangorous, Wagnerian 1.30 p.m. crescendo that heralds seven hundred odd publicans' porters crashing open the gates of seven hundred odd public houses, from the halls of Chapelizod to the shores of Irish town, from the *beaumonde* of Dun Laoghaire to the commonalty of Larkhill.

That tranquil Dublin Sabbath moment   *81*

Up to the thirsty, envious plains of Fingal it crashes. Down to the parched, covetous hills beyond the Featherbed it rolls, proclaiming to all lesser breeds without the law that big brother from Dublin, with little brother from Dun Laoghaire, is moving in again for his Sunday pre-prandial pint. The great thirst is over; the great gargle has begun.

Is it necessary, this Sunday pre-prandial? In the old days, when the barriers did not go down until two o'clock and rose again at five, there was no necessity because there was no opportunity. But necessity knows no logic, and once a man gets the habit of the pre-prandial pint, he can never hope to eat again without it, even if he has to stand about in rain and sleet to wait for it.

Stand about he must. Dublin wives, well-seasoned in the battle of the Sunday licensing hours, appreciate the value of the surprise attack, and are as slick as conjurors in their approach. A moment too long in the armchair; a second's play too long with the chisler, and FLASH:—the stuff is on the table, steaming, unbearably tempting. GET OUT: Get Out at all costs, for the tradition of it is that, if the stuff comes up before you get out, you have had your quietus in the battle, and must eat unlubricated.

So arises the Dublin Sunday phenomenon of the waiting hour, when numerous male citizens can be observed loitering aimlessly through the noonday city, each one looking like a lost soul.

Observe the different manners of their waiting. See the respectable *petit bourgeois*, standing at a respectable distance from his paradise, trying hard not to look at it, while his every nerve quivers for the melodious crash of its concertina gate.

Or observe the bolder sons of the proletariat; nonchalant, backs glued to the pub walls, affectionate human buttresses of its beloved facade. No timidity there. 'We're here,' they seem to say, 'because we're here and hump the begrudgers.'

Or, more subtle perhaps, the sportsmen wandering in the nearby parks, one eye watching the players, the other eye watching the minutes.

Or, most admirable of all, those patrician characters who never seem to arrive, but just manifest themselves at the appropriate moment. Even as the walls of Jericho fell before Joshua's trumpet, so do the publicans' gates fall before their appearance. 'Seek not to know,' they seem to say, 'for whom the gates crash open. They crash open for us.'

So it goes on; 1.30 to 3 o'clock when a decent man should be at lunch; 5 o'clock to 7 o'clock when a decent man should be at tea. Frantic curates, babel of orders, up the pumps and down the hatches, racing the clock, digestion in ruins, roast in cinders, wife in hysterics, chislers in tears. One little hour earlier opening in the afternoon, two little hours later opening in the evening; and the family might actually behold the face of the bread-winner at Sunday mealtimes. The Family, says the Constitution, is the thing. Not by the antic minds that framed the Sunday licensing laws it isn't.

... Ah yes, Madam, a question ... A woman's question, if I may say so, Madam ... Why not, you ask, lay in a stock and save all this rushing, all this waiting?

I tried it myself one week, Madam, half a dozen home on Saturday night in a brown paper bag. They are still waiting there for me, and I am still waiting at my Sunday corner, discreetly obscured by one of the most respectable Sunday journals . . . . it's not the same stuff, Madam, when you remove it from its setting.

And anyway, it would be an un-Irish thing to do, and the true Irishman would have more respect for his family than to do it. What: Drinking it there in his own home in front of the wife and the chislers? Why, it's like something pagan, something indecent, something that only a—a—Frenchman or one of those queer foreign fellows would be thinking of doing.

The Lawng Chrissamas Decorations

Every townsman to his own taste. In September the Cockney takes his old Dutch to the hop-fields for the hop-picking. In December the Jack takes his oul' bird to the kerb-side for any pickings that happen to be going. Even as the shop windows of the professionals go all a-glitter with silver snow, the two-floor backs of the amateurs go all a-bustle with preparations for the annual Christmas selling spree. But though the Kent fields welcome the Cockney, the Dublin streets take a guarded view of the kerb-side trader.

Among the big streets, Henry Street is today the only one prepared to let her hair down for Christmas, and let rip with kerb-side carnival. Time was when both Henry Street and George's Street kept open house for the dealers all the year round. Then came the clean sweep of 1936. The maidens of the Liberties were lifted, kicking and screaming defiance, from their ancestral thrones and banished back to Camden Street and up to Thomas Street. George's Street, old Scrooge, never let them back; but Henry Street, that true northside democrat, relented, and gave them the month of December for their own.

It was, in a sense, a gesture to her origins. Henry Street, the street of the

Coliseum, the penny bazaar, the waxworks, the Saturday night buskers and minstrels, had always been a traditional street of the dealers. Its vanished hinterland, from the junk-and-bedsteads of Cole's Lane to the fruit-and-fish of Moore Street, with the boots and shoes and clothes of Anglesea market, and the now disappeared empty ghost-town shanties fronting Horseman's Row and Norfolk Market, was once a little boom town in itself. The December concession is therefore but a just tribute from the wealthy new street to the ghost of its once-thriving quarter.

Although the concession covers the month of December, the market does not get into full cry until the fortnight before Christmas. The full-time dealers come early, but the amateurs have to undergo a month's austere abstinence from pub and pictures before sufficient capital is raised to purchase a stock. They purchase from wholesalers as they get the readies saved, dealing for the most part in paper chains, balloons and small toys. Their assets as traders are good lungs and unlimited stamina; their liabilities a ready generosity, and a congenital aversion to keeping money in a purse.

One side of the street only is supposed to be open to selling. The bulk of the sellers are not recognised stall-holders, as are the aristocrats of Moore Street. The Law permits them to sell, but not to sit down to their selling. The use of tables or stationary fixtures is forbidden. Some use baskets slung around their shoulders. Others use upended boxes or adopt the happy evasion of fixing trays to fit precariously on one leg, the assumption being that anything standing on one leg cannot legally be deemed a table.

Much of the kerb-side dealing in Henry Street today is a family affair. Some of the Moore Street dealers will desert their fruit stalls for the month; and an occasional cultured hand will condescend to gyrate a jumping monkey as a holiday from concealing an elusive queen. For the rest it is Father, Mother and the Family in three-part harmony. Mother looks after the cash; father guards the claim and moves up and down the scene replenishing or exchanging stock; while the family drone, a dignified statue of leisure, drapes himself with the paper chains, holds aloft the big balloons, and for his part just stands and waits.

For years the Henry Street strip was sacred to the ladies of the north side of the river, and there was not much pressure on space. Then the dealers of Thomas Street began to sniff the promise of loot and lucre in the air, and from their hill quarters across the river they descended into the fertile plains. Like Slattery's Light Dragoons they came, five-and-fifty oul' wans and a number of stout gossoons, carrying billy-cans, tea-pots, and provender for a long day's standing.

There was a time when such an invasion would have set the old traditional

An aristocrat of Moore Street and the Chrissamas balloons

spleen that exists between North and South erupting. But for a miracle, skin and hair did not go flying all over O'Connell Street. The challenge was met with peaceful fortitude. First come first served for the best pitches, decided the local ladies—and the local ladies had not so far to come.

Space on the most valuable part of the strip, the section between Moore Street and the Pillar, became as precious as gold claims in the old Yukon. Morning claiming-time moved back from eight, to seven, then to six o'clock; and finally, for the last few valuable days before Christmas, the local families who held rights on the best pitches were taking it turn about to do an all-night standing on their sites in order to preserve them from usurpation or take over.

The balloons go up; the toy trumpets blow; the voices peal, 'Get the last a the jumpin' monkeys . . . get yer lawng Chrissamas decorations!' Yet the days of the easy pickings are over. Too many dealers are chasing too few customers. Who cares—as long as there is a few bar left over for the Christmas dinner, enough to fill the paper bags on Christmas Eve, a Hopalong suit for the chisler? It's all part of a tradition, the Jack's annual holiday from leisure.

Shopkeepers look on and wonder. Year after year they decide that something should be done about it. How can their customers get in through the milling throng?

Then, wise men. they figure the other side of the question. Once safely in, how can their customers ever get out again?

On the Outside—Looking In

We who hang around the railings and main gates of Dublin Castle and Iveagh House and the Pro-Cathedral, attending the great occasions of State and Church and Social Life from the outside looking in, are, as a class, pretty well bad news with everybody. The Gardai itch to move us along; the organisers of things view us with concern; the Press, when it refers to us at all, dismisses us with the grudging and inaccurate statement that 'crowds began to gather at an early hour'.

Yet we take no umbrage at this horrible misnomer. For we are not just any old crowd. We are always the same crowd, the epicures of great events, and we are to ordinary crowds as gourmets are to men who bolt mixed grills at snack-bars. They rush up and gulp the great event and go home afterwards suffering from mental indigestion. We make a nine-course dinner of the occasion; the first Garda on the beat in the morning is our anticipatory apéritif; the last paper bag blowing over the emptied street at night is our final, lingering port.

We are old in the history of great events. The Greeks dramatists knew us well, and used us as a chorus. The Caesars knew our value, and used to treat us right royally with circus and with triumph. Shakespeare knew us too in those ubiquitous citizens of his, First, Second, and Third, who, whenever there were awkward questions to be asked or impertinent remarks to be

Dignitaries of State

addressed, were always there for the asking or the addressing. Without us Mark Anthony would have been but a voice crying in the wilderness, and Francois Villon a singer without a lyre to play upon.

Yet we are not loved. *Odi profanum vulgus* began one of our earliest critics, and his descendants mock at us today when they catch us at our all-night sittings outside Buckingham or the Elysée Palace. But we do not come to these places in the early hours of the morning for the tawdry purpose of being photographed as first in a queue. We are there because we are the natural

The natural long-nosed ones of the world

long-nosed ones of the world, our function in history being to keep tabs on the doings of our betters.

You will always know us when you see us. We are like well-bred pointers on the game, nose forward, limbs frozen into immobility. We have only two restrictions. No man may join us of the type who rushes up demanding . . . 'Wha's going on, aye?' For a true brother or sister of our company it is enough to know that there is *SOMETHING* going on. Neither may a man join us who has permitted himself to become too much of a somebody. It is not that we think the less of a man for being a somebody; it is only that, sooner or later, we know the crowd inside the railings will discover his presence amongst us, and they will send out for him and drag him in, and his fate will depress us terribly.

For we know that the best view of things is the outside view. We can look in at them and reflect; they can only look at one another and compare. They may have to drink sweet and tiny liqueurs for which nature never designed their palates. We can go back to the pub and drink great flowing pints. They are like people who have climbed a mountain only to find that there is nothing left but higher more tantalising mountains; we are still sitting at the foot of the mountain, speculating as to what is at the top. They can claim, and with truth, that they are the wheels without which our world could not move; we can claim that we are the brakes without which the wheels might rush on to destruction.

We are a great crowd for knowing who everybody is. We know all the backgrounds and have all the skeletons taped. We will stand with equal patience for presidents or pontiffs or film stars, but our greatest thrill is when those we know by personal acquaintance pass in. We may pass such a one in the street any day without regard for him, but we will surge forward to see him on this particular day, just because he is wearing his sash or his medal or his chain of office. Maybe this is because we feel that he is a brother gone wrong . . . 'I knewn that fella,' we murmur, 'when he hadn't a tosser.' Yet we do not murmur it in envy or spite. Rather is it with us a sort of melancholy pride that, through all the vicissitudes of our own lives, we have somehow managed to avoid the same tosser.

It is good for us that this should be so. We who are the makers of revolutions can hardly consider the guillotine for a man whose only crime it is that, since we left him at the school gate, he has managed to salt away a few tosser. Besides, if he is in the palace tonight, he might be back in the pub tomorrow, and it would be embarrassing to meet him then, after having harboured designs upon his neck.

I am sure it is good for them too. There must be many a solid dignitary of

Church and State today who, on his way into a great event, can suddenly be brought up short with memories, as he sees, in the beaming lineaments of some oul' wan of our company, the features of the older girl who used to take him by the hand to school at Strand Street or the Brunner. That keeps him on a good level, and to a proper size—and ensures that the only barrier between us is the harmless barrier of a railings.

Abroad is where you find it

The best man for the blues, the sharpest shot for the old mental reflexes, is a change of scene. I do not mean the Alps or the Balearics, though these places are all very well in their way. I was thinking rather of the lane that runs back of my garden, which in ten years' residence I have never bothered to explore; the by-road which winds from your house to the city, and which in twenty years' driving the main road you have never bothered to take.

Such places can snap us right out of our dumps. Yet for most of us they are further away than Peru, and the only time we ever see them is when we get pitched into them by accident. A man can, indeed, get a change of scene if he pays his way to Peru. But he has little to shout about; for he is only getting what he paid for. But a man who can find a change of scene outside his door every morning—he is getting his new world for nothing, and has really something to be talking about.

Thus I envy children; they are the only true explorers. To their anticipatory, eager eyes every street corner is an adventure, every garden wall a challenge. We snap at them when out walking because they must be up every blind alley and down every hole in the road. And we forget the buoyant days of our own childhood, when every hole in the wall was an opening to goblin-land, every curtained window a screen for cabalistic goings-on.

Sometimes we are lucky and Providence, realising that we are not wholly depraved, gives us a break. So one morning our regular road is torn up, our bus is rerouted from the broad highway to the narrow street. Then we look up startled, from our morning ration of war and rumour, to discover that we are sailing along through strange country, the sun is shining on old brown bricks, men, dogs, houses and horses have resumed their three dimensions again, and we are, through no merit of our own, *alive*.

In such manner I myself, arriving into town the other morning not long back from holiday, and thinking what a dull, dead, stale and unprofitable

That canny breed of half-town, half-country

dump it was to be sure, was hailed by a citizen who was belting over Smithfield way in pursuit of a second-hand piano for his chislers.

Forbearing to ask what a second-hand piano should be doing in that place of fodder men and merchant men, I walked with him down a drab street, turned into a laneway, and ended up in a tumbledown shed by a cobbled yard where a man sold fodder. Fodder and a second-hand piano. It stood there, with straw sticking out of it, surrounded by bales of hay, cart-wheels and half a motor chassis.

Why? Why was the fodder man selling a second-hand piano? I dared not ask him, for all of a sudden I knew I was back in the foreign lands of childhood again, where it is not matter for comment that things should go bump in the morning, or mysterious fodder men conjure ancient pianos out of bales of hay.

The fodder man did not explain. 'O'ny ting I know about this piano,' he said, 'is that it's worth fifteen quid.'

We bought his piano and went out to drink with him in a fusty little pub that I swear he must have conjured up too, for in years of walking those parts I had never seen it before. There were other horse-and-cart men there, travelling men with old coats tied across the middle with sugawns. They were the last of the free men, of that canny breed of half-town, half-country, knocking it out the hard way between back lanes in cities and back doors in villages, fighting a gallant rearguard action against the soul-deadening security of the weekly pay packet. Someone offered a 'clatter' of ducks cheap. Someone had an 'oul' bowler' outside and did anyone want him for nothing? When I left, it was with regret, for at any moment I expected someone else to arrive, shoulders covered with a canvas bag, middle tied up with rope, to offer us a brace of tigers from Rathangan or a 'clatter' of elephants from Kilcock.

Well, what a tomfoolery, you say, about a couple of jobbers and a couple of yokels in a back lane pub. But wait! I thought I *knew* this neighbourhood. And all the time I only knew its face. And you think you know your avenue, and all the time you only know what it shows you. It is not the faces of houses that tell you things, it is their back yards; and of a sudden I was shamed by the number of places there are in Dublin to which I have never been.

I had never been on the lower deck of a bus, except to stand uneasily on the platform. And yet to a man who ordinarily travels top deck in a bus there can be nothing more utterly 'abroad' than the lower deck. There are strange foreign people down there, leading lives which we mere males glimpse in passing but of which we really know nothing; housewives with shopping-bags and a strange jargon all their own, telling stories of villainous butchers and evil grocers, and wrestling with urgent problems of food prices and clothes prices, which to me are only figures in a newspaper.

Or what can be more 'abroad' to a man who only knows the city in its lunch-time rush than the city when it wears its leisurely, feminine, eleven-o'clock mantle? Or what a change of scene it would be for the broker who only knows Dame Street by day to walk out some white night of moonlight into its cold, chaste, silent, two-o'clock-in-the-morning emptiness, where for once in his life he could hear the strange exotic sound of his own feet upon the pavement.

So I mused, walking away from the cobbled yard and the piano with straws in it and the 'clatter' of ducks and the half-country, half-town men to whom no street of Dublin, no parish of Ireland is not known. And my friend must have felt so too, for, as we turned a còrner into what Joyce describes as 'the dull inelegance of Capel Street', he suddenly threw his hand at it as though he suspected it to hold all the secrets of Baghdad.

'You know,' he opined, 'but it's a quare, corny, mixed-up class of an oul' town all the same.'

And so it is, and some year I must go to my native city for a holiday.

Hark, Hark, the Nark

You can always tell that spring is coming to Dublin when you see the public speaker moving back to the corner of Abbey Street for his outdoor season. He is as regular to his platform there as is the spring swallow to its gilded eaves; and his citizens' forum, with its party men, its preventers of things and its promoters of things, is a requisite part of the evening's entertainment for rubbernecks who do not like going home at night.

There is nothing diffident about the public speaker's arrival to the Abbey Street forum. First he greets you with the strains of martial music. Then, over the roof-tops, echoes the peal of his high-pitched heroic voice, his ringing tones invoking visions of Bastilles falling and barricades rising. It sounds like a prelude to Armageddon, or a resurrection of Meagher of the sword; but when you get there it is nothing worse than a mild little man discoursing into a truculent microphone.

This citizens' forum is a very necessary aid to the peace in a country where the only man not born to be an orator is the man born to be a heckler. The public speech and the organisation are to an Irishman what the song and the choir are to a Welshman; and political party leaders become painfully aware

Born to be an orator

of this fact at election times, when they discover that the average supporter, however dubious he may be about lending his car or his money to the cause, has no hesitation whatsoever about lending his voice.

Fortunately there is no lack of academies for the training of the novice speaker. There are as many organisations for the promotion and prevention of things in this town as there are things to prevent and promote. You see little of them in winter except a rash of posters on walls, or a series of indoor debates where conservatives go all out for the prevention of the preventers.

In spring, however, the committee rooms and the indoor meetings close up, and the real work of public speaking gets under way. Now, with the older politicians going out of business, the Abbey Street forum may yet become as important a source of replacement to the Dail of tomorrow as the Oxford Union once was to the House of Commons.

Up to recently the majority of the speakers in the organisations have been countrymen resident in Dublin. The Jack, although one of the world's natural speechmakers, is too good-natured and indolent a citizen to be of much use in the prevention or promotion of things. When he does try, he always ends up by getting everything slightly wrong.

You will notice him hanging round the door of the indoor function, trying to give the impression that he has just happened along by accident, and asking irrelevant questions. If the meeting has to do with International Affairs, he will want to know its outlook on old horses. If it has to do with old horses, he will demand a full statement on its policy towards Anti-Partition. This does not endear him to the organisers who are, for the most part, single-minded men.

Outside, however, the Jack is coming more into favour, mainly because of the great change that has occurred in public speaking over the past year. In other years the favourite subject of meetings has always been Empire and its iniquities, and the Jack is not hot on Empire and its iniquities. He tries hard, but deep inside him there still glows a traditional regard for the raj and the imperial purple and the Dublin fusiliers, and this gives an equivocal note to his approach.

The drunks who come bothering the forum after closing-time are not men to be silenced by the voice of indecision, and the Jack has never had much chance to impress by comparison with the piercing intensity of the Northmen or the great rolling gutturals of the Burren.

Now, with the era of the denouncement going out, and the era of the nark coming in, the Jack has his big chance. The Dublin adenoid is the finest and most plaintive instrument ever devised. It may be weak on the iniquities on Empire, but it is superb on the price of the pint, and because of that quality it is yet going to be the saviour of the art of public speaking in Ireland.

For there is no doubt that the public speaker is losing his grip. Audiences are gone to other pastimes. The torchlight processions are few. The tar barrels are dead and empty. The ebullient microphones are screaming to deserted villages, and only the few faithful rubbernecks remain at the street corners. It was not thus, say the old-timers sadly, with Healy and O'Brien, who had no mikes at all.

Meanwhile, audience or no, the speakers stick to their task. Is an audience, they seem defiantly to ask, really necessary? Once I saw a famous politician addressing a meeting in Smithfield. His audience consisted of a drunk, three oul' wans and a gang of chislers. The drunk kept informing him mournfully that 'we're a horrid bog country'; the oul' wans discussed his antecedents in familiar tones; the chislers tried to set fire to his platform. He meanwhile deluged them with a full flow of his statistics, as contented as though he were addressing the Federation of Irish Manufacturers.

And that is, perhaps, the secret of the true public speaker. He does not really care about his audience. Like the lyric poet and the nightingale, he sings because he must.

Outside Influences

Go Home, Punctuality Men

What's wrong with Dublin today is that there's too much punctuality and do-it-nowism knocking around. There are too many Limeys at large in this town, all single-minded citizens with a strong reluctance to put off until after Christmas anything that can be done today. Mucking up our traditional ways of not getting things done they are, and undermining our immemorial privileges of not having anything very much to do.

Me, I am not against the English businessman; I am only against having to do business with him. Observed attending to his business in his native habitat (watching pretty little business ladies playing net-ball in Lincoln's Inn Fields, or heckling the park corner orators of the neighbourhood), the English businessman seems much like the sort of decent, harmless God-Send-Sunday tycoon that we breed ourselves—and by all the accounts of his English press critics that's exactly what he is.

But transferred to Dublin, where the local business day probably seems to him like an eight-hour luncheon with occasional pauses for work between courses, the Englishman becomes all too conscious of his heritage as a son of Empire and Efficiency. If he makes an appointment, he keeps it; if he writes a letter, he expects an answer to it.

The last time I got a letter from a newly appointed English agent (about some account which was in dispute for a mere matter of only two years) I promptly, as is my wont, lost the thing. A week later I got a second letter, couched in most peremptory fashion, and concluded with a sentence of shocking rudeness. '*Kindly*,' demanded the concluding sentence, '*acknowledge receipt of this communication.*'

The preposterous demand so jolted my sensitivities that instead of losing the communication outright I stuck it in my special pocket where I keep all the more distasteful communications of the sort that go . . . *Dear Sir . . . unless this matter . . . within seven days . . . hands of our law agent . . .* and to which I never reply on principle.

Five days passed, and then I ran into my churlish correspondent in Henry

Street. To my cordial salute he returned a cold Britishy look, 'I say, look here,' he complained, 'you never acknowledged my communication.'

I led him gently to the nearest friendly local licensed premises. 'This,' I explained, 'is where communications are best acknowledged in this town.' We parted later in the morning, nicely primed for lunch and full of appreciation of each other's point of view. Admittedly the matter in dispute has not been settled yet, but now we meet every month to settle the thing and some day, no doubt, we shall.

In the meantime my friend has learned to receive acknowledgements of his communications in the proper Dublin way and in the proper Dublin places, and is greatly admired by all the people in his London office (except his accounts department) for the manner in which he has won Irish customers and influenced Irish sales.

But, while you can sometimes convert the Englishman from his business methods, you cannot divert him from his uncivilised approach to our business or political associations. Englishmen do not understand that one of the chief goods and purposes of Irish associations is oratory, not action. They do not understand that passing resolutions is one thing, having to *do* something about them is another. They do not understand that most questions on the agenda at Irish meetings are there not for being settled, but for being argued about. They do not understand that any question *really* intended to be settled at an Irish meeting never appears on the agenda at all, for the very good reason that it is always settled before the meeting opens.

We used to have a lovely association down my quarter of which, by reason of my well-known proficiency at messing-up minutes and ignoring resolutions and forgetting to forward condemnations, I was elected hon. secretary. We used to have wonderful times, coming in hours late, ignoring the agenda and interrupting the chair. We used to issue condemnations of the Board of Works, admonish the ESB, threaten the City Manager, discuss the Middle East and the four-minute mile, and make indignant demands on every Coras in the business to have delegations of our members received forthwith or else. All this the meeting used to do in the happy security of the realisation that the hon. secretary could be trusted to forget every decision five minutes after he had been instructed to implement it.

Then the Limey came. He turned up at the appointed hour for the meeting and was left standing outside for half an hour in the rain. We felt so bad about it that we elected him to our first delegation of the night, a pressure quintet that was scheduled to call upon and castigate the City Management on the following Monday.

Heavens! Not alone did the man turn up at the City Hall the following

Monday but, after waiting three hours for the rest of us, he finally decided to call on and castigate the City Management himself, and discovered that not alone had the City Management never heard from us, but that the City Management had never even heard of us. Now we are afraid to condemn even CIE.

And this sort of thing is bursting out all over. Worse; for not alone are alien influences making our businessmen punctual, they are also making our tradesmen precipitate. Gone is the ancient, dungaree-clad philosopher, dishonest as his tongue was long, turning up three weeks after you had sent for him in emergency, willing to discuss any topic with you except the cost of his materials and time for the job in hand. In his place arrives today, before you have even sent for him, a go-getter in a smart suit and a smarter car, telling you in clipped, efficient accents that, according to what he noticed the other day in passing, your walls are due to fall down or your timber is suffering from dry-rot, and then producing a carefully calculated and *honest* estimate in which everything is priced to a penny and timed to a second.

A plague on them all. They make one feel that there is grave danger of the world ending tomorrow, and that if one does not string along with their systems and their estimates one is going to be caught with one's accounts unsettled, one's books unbalanced, one's premises unrepaired. They take all the uncertainity, all the speculation, out of business.

Do you know what it is; they take all the *pleasure* out of business.

Gentlemen—Our Guests

There was a time, down our quarter, when a man could have a pint on a June evening without having to run the risk of being tainted by 'harmful foreign influences'. We knew that such a thing as the British Tourist existed, but it did not exist much where we imbibed.

A well-spoken, tweedy sort of person we sometimes encountered, temporarily strayed out of the luxurious hostelries south of the river. Intoxicated, he might sometimes suit his humour to our ways. Sober, he would shudder at us as though at something one degree removed from the juke-box. Either way we did not greatly care. His people were not our people; his ways were not our ways. We let him go his way, to fish the untroubled waters of the west, and thought no more about him.

Then, just after the war, a new and shattering element erupted in our midst. Stout, strident, uninhibited, he came to us with his white linen shirt open at the neck, and white canvas shoes walking sacrilegiously down Sackville Street. With him, or more often floundering heavily in his wake, would come his consort. We never saw one without the other. Sometimes they came in pairs, sometimes in convoys, but always laughing heartily and addressing themselves and everybody else as 'Luv'.

At first we did not, as they used to say in the locality, 'appreciate the effort'. In the ethics of our community at that time a man was not supposed to bring his wife into a pub with him, except maybe on Sundays, bank holidays, wakes or weddings. So we tried to ignore them, but they refused to be ignored. An indomitable people, they did not even seem to realise that they were being ignored. Then we gathered in corners and whispered to each other that they were only over to enjoy our steaks and laugh at our ways. They retaliated by enjoying our company and laughing at our jokes. With the passage of the years and the return of plenty, gaps began to appear in the ranks: but the faithful ones are still coming, not for the steaks now but for the humour of it, and we have now learned to accept them on their own terms.

Not alone are they accepted; they are eagerly anticipated; and we learn to mark the months of our summer by the accents of the different arrivals. We always know the season has opened when we hear the Scots, who start trickling in around the June time of year. Blood brothers they are, with their tweed caps and their love of sporting talk and good whiskey.

They are our publican's chosen people, too; for in spite of what the books say about them they are great spenders, and have heads of iron.

If the Scot has a wife, you do not see her much, and you hear her not at all. With him there are serious matters always waiting for discussion, like what do we think of Hibs and Rangers and 'Coltic', and the superiority of 'Fewtball' north of the Tweed. In his stern unecumenical philosophy there are no such nice distinctions and equal denominations as Soccer, Rugby and Gaelic. There is 'Fewtball', which is the true religion, and after it the various heretical sects of the handlers' codes.

But if the Scot is limited and tends to sit in a corner, the 'Luvs' of Lancashire are all-embracing and extend all over the furniture. They drink light ales and are temperate. Publicans accept them cheerfully as a social asset but there is no rubbing of the hands. 'The Englishman,' says the publican, 'will sit on his pint of ale like a mother hen on an egg.' and the older publicans think back wistfully to 'that other kind of Englishman' who used to drink whiskey and clip his consonants. Whenever you see a publican observing a two minutes' silence it is invariably to the memory of 'that other kind of Englishman'

If our publican is nostalgic, we are satisfied. There is no condescension in this new kind of Englishman. He does not come to the big hotels but to the small houses in the suburbs, and he takes the last bus home with the rest of us. He is well-tutored, too, and whenever religion or politics creep into the discussion he will permit a studied blankness to spread across his face. If there are one or two other things just as sacred to us that he knows not of, that is not his fault; and the man who, last summer, on being hospitably offered a pint of stout replied, 'That black puddle: That's a lidy's drink that is,' can hardly be blamed for his mistake. Anyway, he was a Cockney and will probably not be missed much.

For us, the most gratifying part of the whole thing is that, as a tourist effort, it is nearly all our own work. It is mostly by word of mouth that the newcomers are attracted. A pair of new faces will appear. Their friends have been here last year and have told them all about it, so they have decided to find out for themselves. To our surprise and gratification we learn that our pub and our doings are relished and discussed in all sorts of unlikely places like Peebles and Kirkintilloch and Clitheroe and Aycliffe. Then at Christmas the cards come, with promises of returns and inquiries about the doings of our more colourful characters.

Anglophobes of long standing are gradually being converted, and a new *entente cordiale* is being established. It is an *entente* without benefit of subsidy, promotion or covenant. Like the GI said to the top brass when asked for his views on promoting friendship between himself and the natives: 'You can't buy friendship—it just happens.'

Bang-Bang and the Dollar Tourist

I was standing at the top of Dame Street, watching a workgang laying pipes in an open drain on Cork Hill. To be precise, they were not exactly laying the pipes, but they were meditating deeply on the subject, and there was every promise—in their intense brooding immobility—that they might get under way before lunch.

Around the workgang a fine concourse of citizens waited, with true-bred Dublin indolence, for the entertainment to start, and I was reflecting how leisured and peaceful it all was, and how civilised by contrast with other hustling and materialistic cities, when a nasal voice, heavily indicative of the Dollar Tourist, shattered my peace.

'Say, Junior,' demanded the voice, 'does anyone *work* in this town?'

Curtly I indicated the city below us. 'Certainly,' I replied, 'down there, Mister, all sorts of men are working. Editors are editing, bankers are banking, brokers are broking . . .'

'That maybe is what you think, Junior,' he barked, 'that's maybe what they tell you.' He stretched out a massive hand. 'See that pile down there?' he asked, pointing to what was visible of the chaste and classic facade of Trinity College.

'Oh, well,' I said, 'that's not exactly typical, you know.'

'It ain't that,' he answered, 'but behind that pile is a ball park where the stoodents play ball. Waal, six months ago I am in this town and I walk in there at three o'clock in the afternoon and what do I see? Thousands of your bankers and your brokers standing round watching the English ball players practising for the Saturday match. Just running round, Junior, and thousands standing around looking at them.'

'It is customary,' I explained, 'on the eve of rugby internationals for gentlemen of the fancy to gather in College Park on the Friday afternoon before the match to observe both teams at practice. A little apéritif before the main event. After all,' I defended, 'you have your Yale and Harvard.'

'Sure we have! But we just go to the match. We don't go sleeping and eating with the guys.'

Shaken but not yet quelled, I said weakly, 'Surely an occasion . . .'

'Nuts,' said the Dollar Tourist. 'It ain't just one occasion with you guys. Down there,' his pendulum of a fist swung towards Westmoreland Street, 'there's a cawfee shop. Yessir! And all morning there's nothing in that cawfee shops but business guys drinking cawfee and yapping.'

'Considering trends and discussing the dollar export drive,' I ventured.

'Not the way I heard it, they wasn't. You answer me, bub,' said this most uncomfortable man, 'When do folks work? How do things get done?'

It was a question, I knew, that had to be carefully answered. It was important (or so we were continually being reminded) that the tourist should be given a new, true image of us. Efficient: Punctual: Hard-working: SANE.

And then, even as I groped for the right words to explain how things got done, handicapped as I was by the fact that I had not myself the remotest idea, there came a diversion. Down from the direction of the Liberties came sounds of a distant battle drawing nearer; shouts, screams, and a prevailing repetitive Bang-Bang. Then, suddenly rounding Christchurch Place into Lord Edward Street and pursued, in full cry, by hundreds of juvenile followers from Meath Street and the Coombe, appeared the galloping figure of Dublin's best-loved citizen.

He was dressed in his customary attire, a long, musty-green overcoat stretching almost as far as his tattered shoes. From a leathery little dark face his eyes beamed antic love on all the world. His coal-black hair, in an absurd Hitlerite quiff, fell to and fro on his forehead with every hop, step and jump of his gait. His right hand was clenched to the shape of a revolver, the index finger forming the barrel. With it he blazed madly, Bang-Bang! at every passer-by, and every passer-by came alive, laughed, and blazed Bang-Bang! back at him.

Was he a gangster on the run or a cowboy pursued by a posse? In all the years I knew him he never told me, but I think he was a cowboy, for there was a clippety-clop hoppety-hop bounce about his shuffling run that reminded you of Hopalong Cassidy riding fast on the wide prairie. And suddenly from nowhere, up out of the pavement, he used to spring . . .

Bang-Bang! went the running battle down Dame Street.

Bang-Bang! went the followers from behind lamp standards.

Bang-Bang! went the sanitary engineers from their hole in Cork Street.

Bang-Bang! went bus conductors from the backs of their buses.

Bang-Bang! went staid old gentlemen transformed into boys again.

Bang-Bang! went the traffic guard at George's Street, forgetful of dignity.

'Holy Cow,' said the Bronx Boy.

Frightful visions rushed through my mind. This would certainly get to ECA if not to UNO—maybe even into the colums of *Time* itself. As in a dream I could see the banner headlines that would herald another disgrace for Anna Livia Plurabelle: DUBLIN CITIZENS PLAY NOON-DAY COPS AND ROBBERS THROUGH CITY'S MAIN STREETS!

'Not typical,' I said, 'Not at all typical of our sensible city. Just a midsummer day's madness.'

But the American was strangely silent. 'Perhaps,' I said timidly, 'I am keeping you from an important appointment.'

Even as I spoke the clang of metal on concrete gave evidence that the boys on Cork Hill were at last getting to grips with the hole. Across the street two hundred amateur city engineers waited for the operation with keen and critical eyes. I waited for the shattering words that would be my *coup de grâce*.

But they did not come. Forward he took a step; backward he took two steps. 'The heck,' said the Dollar Tourist, 'I ain't watched a good hole in the road since I left my home town.' Then, slightly shame-faced but determined, he walked across the street and humbly took his place in the ranks of the lotus eaters.

Up from the direction of either Grafton Street or Stephen's Green I thought I could hear the faint but triumphant sound of Bang-Bang!

The Pint

Famous Last Words

The defendant, in evidence, said that the night in question, being the opening night of the August holiday week-end, there was an unusually large crowd present. In spite of repeated appeals he had experienced great difficulty in clearing the premises . . .

. . . NOW GENTS NOW GENTS IT'S ON THE TIME NOW GENTS EVERY MAN MAY FINISH HIS GLASS ALL TOGETHER NOW THIS ISN'T A SINGING-HOUSE NO SINGING ALLOWED I SAID PUT OUT THEM LIGHTS CHARLIE . . .

. . . Ah the rare oul' Nedser, that was a luvely song Nedser, a tewer de force Nedser, a classical number that was. Aye will yez ask yer man wid the accordeon to give Nedser an accominiment wid his next . . . Never mind that oul' bags behind the counter . . . What's he talkin' about? . . . Thar's ten minutes before closin' time . . . That clock is fast I tell ya that oul' bags always has the clock fast . . .

. . . AYE AYE AYE Will yiz give a little bit of proper order down that corner Mr. Burren is going to do his number up hyar wan voice now best of order for Mr. Burren . . .

. . . Lissen John: wait'll I tell ye thar he was the bleedin' oul' bowler seven lengths a the field the sun mewen an' stars between him an' the rest a the bleedin' bowlers lissen what does he do the bleedin' bowler down he flops over the last huggle twenty-five brick down the swannee over the last huggle the bleedin' oul' bowler an' me going to Galway wid the missus a Monday. Lissen John; could ye—I mean what way are ye fixed at all—I mean ye know me that's wan ting about me I never ask only . . .

. . . NOW GENTS NOW GENTS IT'S GONE FIVE MINUTES OF THE TIME NOW GENTS FINISH UP THEM GLASSES NOW GENTS WILL YEZ HAVE A BIT OF RESPECT FOR THE LAW PUT THEM LIGHTS OUT CHARLIE . . .

. . . No! No! No! Now look at it this way . . . I mean, take yew as an Irishman . . . I mean I presume y'are an Irishman . . . No! No! No! I didn't mean that as an insult sure I'd know yer an Irishman be the look of ye. No I mean take yew as an Irishman would yew as an Irishman stand by an' do nothing if Russia cem over hyar in the mornin' . . . yis but I mean take it this way . . . we Irish has always been a fightin' race . . .

. . . Naw d'ye knaow what it is I can't understand the chislers today . . . thar's my young fella at home . . . off wud a sack on his back, him an' a half a dozen a the pals. Down ta Kerry thar goin'! *Jaysus man down ta Kerry!* I said to him would yez not go off straight an' proper to Blackpewl or the Isle A Man an' not be traipsing off to them foreign places . . .

. . . Black-pewl? Lord son I gev up them places years ago. Naw! D'ye know whar I'm going for the holliers? Tew weddins this week and Lough Derg wid the missus the week after. True as I'm sittin' here. Tew weddin's an' Lough Derg wid the missus . . .

. . . NOW GENTS NOW GENTS ALL TOGETHER NOW GENTS I SAID PUT OUT THEM LIGHTS CHARLIE . . .

. . . *Where I sported and plaaaaaaayed,*
Neath each green leafy shaaaaaade,
On de banks of my own luvely Leeeeeeeeeee . . .

. . . Ah lave him, lave him, aren't we all Irish? Isn't he as much entitled to his song as the next man . . . what d'ye mean he's a culchie? A Corkman isn't a culchie. I'm tellin' ya Cork city men is not culchies no more nor us is culchies . . .

. . . ORDER ORDER ORDER will yez show a little respec' down thar will yez give a bit of order for Mr. Burren's number are ye right Mr. Burren?

. . . Lissen John: Is that all right wud yew now John—I mean y'are carryin'—I mean I wouldn't ask ye only for the missus lissen thar I was twenty brick to the good an' I goin' out the gate before the last race an' up comes bleedin' Skinnier an' gives me this bleedin' oul' bowler for the last . . . no lissen don't order any more for me no that's wan ting about me is I always know when I have enough . . . well lissen all right so I'll have wan quick bottle be the neck and finish at that but isn't dat a tarrible story that bleedin' oul' bowler . . .

. . . NOW GENTS NOW GENTS IT'S TEN MINUTES GONE THE TIME WILL YEZ HAVE A LOOK AT WHAT TIME IT IS CHARLIE WILL YE GET THEM GLASSES OFFA THE COUNTER . . .

. . . NO! NO! NO! d'English has nothin' to do wud this queskin at all leave d'English outa it altogether. No this is the queskin. Are yew as an Irishman goin' to stand by an' see Russia walkin' in here . . . Look never mind about fighting on the same side as them, look we can't always be bringing up old sores . . . All right for the six counties . . . I care about the six counties too . . . Look I'm jest as good an Irishman as any of yewez goin' round like ye were

Closing-time

dug outa the Republican plot . . . Look I didn't say ye weren't an Irishman
. . . Look I was only making a rhetorical queskin . . . All right, well I'm not in
dread of yous if it comes to that . . . All right take off your coat if you want to
have a go . . . I'll have a ging at ye, yer not all that humpin' big . . .

. . . NOW GENTS NOW GENTS WILL YEZ MIND THEM GLASSES
WILL YEZ GET THAT PAIR OF CANISTERS OUTA HERE BEFORE
THEY WRECK THE PLACE MIND THEM GLASSES PUT ON THEM
LIGHTS CHARLIE . . .

. . . No but lissen John I'm tarrible grateful for them readies the missus'll
have a few bar comin' outa the diddly when we get back an' I'll be able to fix
ye up outa that no that's wan ting about me John I always pays me debts . . .
lissen we'll just have wan more for the road now this wan is on me. Lissen
barman give us tew stouts by the neck in a hurry . . . lissen whadd'ya mean
I've had enough already I know when I've had enough without any bleedin'
culchie tellin' me . . . no we don't want yer opinion we just want tew stouts be
the neck . . . no hould on John I'll teach this culchie . . . go on an' ring yer
three nines . . . no hould on John that's wan ting about me I always know me
rights . . .

. . . ORDER ORDER thar for Mister Burren's number right Mister
Burren yer on Mister Burren don't mind that oul' bags behind the counter
Mister Burren . . .

> *. . . A bunch a the boys wus whooping it up,*
> *In the Malemute saluwen*
> *An' the kid that handled the mewsic box*
> *Was play' a rag-time tuwen*
> *Back a the bar . . .*

. . . GENTLEMEN: GENTLEMEN: THE LAAAAAAAW . . .

*The Justice said that under no circumstances could he accept defendant's excuse, which
he regarded as so feeble as to be almost contempt of court (laughter). It was the duty of the
licensee to have his premises cleared within a reasonable period of closing-time, and he
failed to see the slightest reason for defendant's failure to fulfill his obligation in this
respect. The holiday spirit, said the Justice, amidst further laughter, is not a valid defence
in law . . .*

Reflections

The Four-Legged Fellas

'Them four-legged fellas,' says my friend the horse driver, 'is not for eatin'. Them four-legged fellas will be working their passage around this town when all them dirty petrol lorries is dead and gone.'

I like to hope that my friend the horseman might yet be proved right, both for the sake of horses and the sake of towns. For towns and the men in them are letting themselves fall into dread of machines today. We bow and scrape to the machines, and lay expensive asphalt carpets under their feet. We who were once the lords of creation now scuttle like panicked rabbits to the slightest tootle of a supercilious motor horn.

Horses do not fear the machine; they despise it and retard it. Have you never experienced, in a narrow Dublin street, the glorious sight and sounds of a long line of frustrated juggernauts, howling and honking and bleating with rage behind the calm indifferent progress of some stately shire or tough Irish draught? And, having seen, have you not gone away a better braver man, determined in future to stand your ground against the monsters, if not with certitude at least with fortitude?

Machines drive their owners mad, but horses lead their drivers to tranquility. A man sitting behind his nagging twenty-horse-power engine knows nothing but the fret of changing gears and the fever to be roaring into top. But a man sitting behind one wise old draught horse is free of such goads, for a wise draught horse has only two speeds, dead slow and full stop, and if you do not want the one you can put up with the other.

Then, too, the machine, with its repair shops and its ever-ready spare parts, tends to rob man of his birthright of responsibilities. But a horse develops a man's sense of responsibility, for it has no spare parts. 'A hoss,' says my friend the horseman, 'has always to be watched. A hoss is no different to you or me. It can get the colic or pneumonia or its kidneys can go wrong. It can get run down from overwork just like you or me, and need a month or two out on grass just like you or me.'

It is this sense of personal responsibility that makes horsemen into better,

The horses are going from man's life too

Most of all I regret him from funerals

kindlier men than motormen. You will sometimes hear in the suburbs (at least I do in my suburb) a horseman singing on his morning rounds to the lively accompaniment of the clippety-cloppety hooves, the regular rhythms of his swaying van. But who ever heard of a singing motorman? Do they not go round all day in spasmodic fits and epileptic starts, harbouring murderous desires and muttering horrible imprecations?

I know many horsemen and many motormen for, as a jay-walker of long walking, I have managed to come into contact at some stage or other with almost every horse and every lorry that plies between the Phoenix Park and the North Wall. And I know that I would prefer to be nearly killed any day by a horseman that by a motorman.

For if you encounter the motorman afterwards, in a pub at night, he will embarrass you with his unctuous moralisings and his insufferable smugness and self-righteousness at not having knocked you down. But a horseman will (in retrospect at any rate) treat the incident as a little affair among gentlemen, 'Near got ye thar on Butt Bridge today, son,' he will inform you jovially, 'O'ny for oul' Bessie knewn ye for the walking head-case ye are, ye were gone for your tea.'

I regret the passing of the horse from so many of his functions. I regret him from plough, from canal barge, from bread-van, and from post-office van. But most of all I regret him from funerals, for it was there that one saw him at his best.

How little dignity there is today in being trundled off on one's last round-up in a cold swift motor-wagon. How shabby, by comparison with the stately, leisurely four-in-hands, the splendid nodding black plumes, the tall-hatted statuesque coachmen of more spacious days. In those days a funeral was the better part of a day off from work. Today it is an hour off in the morning, with time neither for the recollection of a man's merits on the way up nor for drinking his memory on the way back. I would like to see what Bloom and Power and Martin Cunningham would do with Paddy Dignam's funeral behind a motor-hearse.

But the horses are going from man's life too. Every week my friend the horseman has a new tragedy to tell. Last week the retainers of a mineral water factory took the meat coffin ship; shortly the distinguished servants of a distillery are scheduled for the same journey. My friend the horseman knows them all, not commercially, as useful implements, but individually as good friends . . . 'Thar's oul' Jem, went off in the last batch, and Molly, the mare with the white shanks, the luvilest mare ever appeared on the streets of Dublin . . .' Listening to my friend the horseman, one tends to get impatient with those logical people who ask you what is the difference between the export of horses for slaughter and the export of bullocks.

'For did anywan,' asks my friend the horseman, 'ever knewn a bullock to know dread of anythin'? Did anywan ever seen a bullock to go galloping round a field just because he was enjoying life? Did anywan ever knewn a bullock that was in any ways different from any other bullock? A bullock,' explains my friend the horseman, 'don't know he's gettin' slaughtered, for the reason that a bullock don't hardly know he's alive in the fust place. But hosses know they're alive. Hosses is like us. Hosses is not meant for eating. You'll see; some day they'll be back in Dublin again when all them dirty petrol lorries is dead and gone . . .'

Me and my Shadow

It was in London, some weeks ago, that the idea first occured to me. I had been exploring the West End, hoping for a glimpse of that rare and almost extinct bird, the London Clubman. I had seen many domestic sparrows and a few vivid specimens of the high-crested Edwardian, but it was not until late afternoon, lurking in ambush by a corner off Pall Mall, that I spotted the rarity itself. It was progressing out of St. James's Square, much as the swan in the evening moves over the lake, and as I gazed I thought with deep emotion, 'If this be the London Clubman, then the London Clubman is glorious, indeed.'

In each one of its constituents, gloves, bowler, length of dignified limb, knife-creased pinstripe, and seeming utter indifference to its surroundings, it was exactly as described by all the great ornithologists of its era, from P G Wodehouse down. Tradition, I could see, went to its make-up, breeding, discipline and good tailors. But the very pith, the core, the *essence* of its glory, was the impeccably rolled umbrella by its side. There and then I decided. I would introduce the Impeccably Rolled Umbrella to my baggy-kneed, porter-stained home town. I would introduce it if they killed me for it.

They very nearly did.

I pass lightly over the obvious reactions, the shrinkings of friends, the derisive cries of 'shoneen', 'gligeen', 'West Briton', from enemies. These things are familiar to all non-conformist citizens, from citizens who try to achieve beards to citizens who try to achieve Buddha. No; it is in the pubs that I suffer most keenly. No sooner have I crooked the handle delicately around the edge of the marble than eyebrows are raised, looks exchanged, situations misconstrued. Pleasantries, no doubt, and not meant in malice, but I have not yet acquired the thick skin of the true devotee, and in the ensuing fracas, win, lose or draw, I am invariably blamed by the publican.

'A man,' declares the more reactionary publican type, 'that would bring a yoke like that into a public house must be looking for trouble in the first place.' And it even more painful with the progressives. Secretly, they will murmur their approval, and then hurriedly offer to keep my umbrella behind the bar until such time as I am ready to leave. 'Some of my best friends,' they assure me, 'have umbrellas . . . but . . .'

It would, of course, be easier were the climate more suitable. In London, where even some of the finest days have a dubious or sceptical air about them, the rolled umbrella can be worn without, on the one hand, seeming redundant, or, on the other, having to undergo the indignity of violating its creases. But in Dublin, where days, like opinions, tend to be more dogmatic than speculative, the umbrella becomes a utensil, and is not rolled at all. So the queries begin. If it is sunny, 'Why am I carrying it?' . . . If it is raining, 'Why don't I open it?' . . . 'Is it all right?' . . . 'Am I all right?' . . . Thus the questing looks; and umbrellaless oul' wans in bus queues eye me as though I were some sort of sadistic dog in the manger that not alone prefers getting wet myself but likes to see them getting wet too.

Yet, strangely, it is upon those ordinarily most rabid of enemies, the small boy and the uniformed official, that my umbrella has its finest effects. If I, sans umbrella, attempt to board a moving bus, the conductor will normally address me in plaintive but crude tones, 'Aye mac, d'yez want to get yerself lagged, do yez?' But yesterday, umbrella happily on arm, I hopped a bus in D'Olier Street, and the custodian (of course it may be that all south suburb conductors talk to their customers like this) merely turned reprovingly to me, 'Now, now, sir, we must not do that, must we?'

This is because the Impeccably Rolled Umbrella, with its classic virtues of order, harmony and restraint, is the only surviving relic of our aristocratic past; and small boys and uniformed officials are the only people left with any true sense of the aristocratic. An intrusive urchin, twacked out of your way at a football match with hand or stick, will immediately set up a howling dirge and get you into grave trouble with the populace for that most heinous of all Dublin crimes, 'hitting the other fellow's chisler'.

Poke the brat, however, with an umbrella, and he will remain respectfully mute and, with luck, will maybe even get out of your way. His sense of history defeats him. He may not know it but he senses it; the walking stick is merely the descendant of the shillelagh, conjuring up visions of Ryan Rooskeys and Ryan Ruadhs leathering it out in faction fights on the slopes of Cappamore or

Bilbo; the Impeccably Rolled Umbrella is of the sword, connoting the great city days of the eighteenth century. Buck Whaley would not be ashamed of the Impeccably Rolled Umbrella if he were alive today, nor would those earlier adventurous swordsmen of the Irish Brigade, swaggering it splendidly from Dunkirk to Belgrade.

I think, if ever I am forced by circumstances to adopt a life of crime, I will do so with a rolled umbrella. The Garda, above all other men, are the ones most susceptible to its influence; only the other day a Sergeant called me 'Sir' as I strolled down O'Connell Street, and I do not believe that any other citizen has been so addressed by a uniformed official since the year nineteen hundred and twenty-two.

There may be somewhere, a Garda so raw, so forgetful of tradition, that he would arrest a man found illegally on enclosed premises with a rolled umbrella in his possession. But I do not think that there exists a Justice—High, Circuit, District, or Supreme—who would sentence a man wearing a rolled umbrella in the dock. And if they get me, they cannot take it from me. I am not carrying it; I am *wearing* it. It is just as much a part of my apparel as is my trousers; and even the law is not permitted to leave me, naked, to mine enemies.

Chislers is Bad News

There was a smash of glass, a scampering of feet, and then an old man stuck his head through his broken window-pane. He was not mad about it; you could see that he had become quite accustomed to it. 'Chislers,' he said resignedly, 'is bad news these days.' And he left it at that.

And as far as Dublin is concerned, he had it right. Chislers are taking over the city. They run under your legs in Dame Street, pick your pockets in Grafton Street, sniffle for pennies in O'Connell Street, and throw slap-bangs under the feet of old ladies with weak hearts.

It's all due to this modern cult of the child. In other days people were not expected to like children. You tolerated them unless they obtruded themselves. When you got too much obtrusion, you spanked them and sent them to bed—those of them, that is, who were not already engaged in chimney-sweeping, match-selling in the snow, or being fags at bleak and ferocious public schools. Thus they were never bad news; in fact it did not pay them to be news at all.

Now it is different. Now it is considered nice in one to like children and, while this is a safe enough sentiment in places where they are in short supply, it is very dangerous in a fertile city such as Dublin.

I say—and I speak with the immense authority of a non-parent—it is unnatural to be devoted to chislers. Fair enough if you are a politician on the make; then it is your business, just like having proper sentiments about things, and ultimately you wind up getting something out of it. But it is bad for the ordinary man to have to simulate this modern cult of being in favour of them and thinking well of them.

I knew a man who used to keep a newsagency on the quays, and treat chislers in the nineteenth-century, pre-Spock fashion. One day he came from behind his counter to behold a bratling of eight years old heading rapidly east-due-south with a bundle of his expensive magazines. He followed hotfoot and, as he came in reach, the bratling settled the question by unloading the stuff over the Liffey wall.

My friend yelped in agony as he watched his magazines sinking, at a cost of two shillings a go. Then he caught the chisler one good clip on the ear. There was a scream such as pigs make on their death-bed. 'He hot me! He hot me!' roared the chisler.

Immediately there came flocking around my friend a veritable gaggle of oul' wans, not merely the robust oul' wans of those Liffeyside parts but also passing-by oul' wans with fur coats and posh accents. My friend was called 'an unholy monster', 'a doirty little bully', a ruffian and a coward. He was threatened with the NSPCC, the NSPCA, and with getting 'thrun inta the river'. Finally, when the kid's father arrived he turned out to be a slag of about seventeen stone of dock muscle who had just suffered the agony of seeing a long-odds Yankee fall down on an odds-on favourite and was in a mood to do something about it.

My bookselling friend, now happily out of hospital, has changed completely. If a similar thing were to happen to him today, he would just smile weakly and try to look like a man of liberal principles. 'Boys,' he would simper, 'will be boys.'

There are thousands of adults like him going around today, decent men and women coerced by false principles into being nice to children at all costs. You see them all over, being taken away in vans, muttering wild snatches of Hilaire Belloc's *Cautionary Verses,* and clinging pathetically to little pictures of King Herod. Teachers, shopkeepers, cinema managers and policemen all wear haggard looks; and if you were to investigate their dreams you would find them having visions of a Nirvana where they are locked in a sound-proof, steel-encased room, with a birch in one hand, a gun in the other, hordes of pimply, pasty-faced boys lined up before them howling in a mass Dublin accent . . . and not an oul' wan in sight.

What we need today is a new reactionary movement, a Society For The Protection of Adults Against Chislers, with good old Arnold of Rugby stuff, and no holds barred. It is either that or the coming dictatorship of the juvenile proletariat.

The Boss and the Boy

The way things are going today, with assembly-lines killing off our old craftsmen and electronic computors spreading havoc among the clerks, it would seem that there are only about two occupations left in this town that cannot be touched by either Time or the Machine. One is the occupation of Boss, who alone can afford to meet Time as an equal; the other is the occupation of Boy, who alone can afford to despise it as an inferior.

For whatever science may invent in future to save time and deracinate labour, there must always remain, in every concern from grocery shops to government buildings, one person at the top making the decisions, and another person at the bottom making a mess of the decisions.

The machines can fill in the gaps between, but the manager and the messenger must seal off the ends; and the comfort of it is that, while modern knowledge has given the boss power to explode atoms at the push of a button, ancient wisdom has never taken from the boy his instinct to mess things up by pushing the wrong button.

The Boy is an old as Original Sin, and can never be expendable. Behind that grimy and anonymous facade, known in every business in the town by his professional title of 'HEY YOU', is the spirit of Puck, without which our human comedy would never have reached the end of its first act. His university is the street; his teaching in philosophy the kicks and cuffs of his betters; his modern language course the curses of despatch managers; and his diploma the invaluable street secrets of survival against the odds.

If I were a king, I would have a cabinet of messenger-boy graduates. I would force every youth, fresh from school or college, to undertake a six month's course riding a fully-laden bike between Thomas Street and Talbot Street. Many a brash young blade, festooned with certificates on every subject, would I civilize with a parcel-laden push over Butt Bridge on a windy March day. Many a conceited classic scholar, free and easy with his Horatian

The town crier of the modern world

odes, would I see the better of a clip in the ear from some uncouth but muscular despatch clerk, whose Latin studies had never gone beyond the elementary information that all Gaul is divided into three parts.

Such a youth would soon learn a wisdom that the schools do not always teach. He would learn that a fight between two dogs in a street can be more entertaining and instructive than a fight between two heroes in a Greek myth. He would learn that the longest way round on fine summer afternoons is, if not the most economic way home for his employer, the most wholesome way home for himself. With the world's governments staffed by such messenger-boy graduates, the world would soon be a safer place to live in. Then wars would be fought by cabinets at fist range, and everybody would be ten minutes late for everything.

In a world where the people lived by the messenger boy's code of unpunctuality there would be no possibility of waging a major war; and in a world where everybody needs as little out of life as a messenger boy there would be no possible reason for starting one. The idealistic nationalist and the realistic grabber are the boys who start the big fires burning; a citizen whose needs can be satisfied by a one-and-one at the chipper, and whose ideals have never been stimulated by the hate-cults that pass for school histories, could be trusted to play his wars on a personal level, and in a minor key.

Then, if I taught sense to the school scholars, I would teach Latin to the street scholars. It is a mistake to undervalue the intellectual and and artistic capacities of the messenger boy. They may look like a prime collection of thugs and potential muggers, but if you take the trouble to investigate you will find that the indomitable skulls carry within them a fascinating variety of interests. I have discovered old Dublin street historians (most of the history not suitable for polite records), breeders of canaries, experts on terriers, catchers of rats, painters on glass, Al Jolsons by the dozen, Frankie Laines by the score.

They all have this in common; they are all cheerful, all unpunctual. They are the town criers of the modern world, fearlessly prepared to hold up the dynamo of industry and commerce while they carry their tit-bits of street gossip from one house of business to the next. I have never known an efficient one yet, but it is from them I have learned most of whatever useful knowledge I possess.

It may be that the world will never have the sense to submit its destinies to leaders who possess the messenger boy's capacity for being in love with life; but, if the boy can never become the boss, it is a relief to think that the boss can never do without the boy.

For the real reason for the messenger boy's existence is not the bearing of messages. It is rather the bearing of all the accumulating narks of the day as they make their snowballing way down from top to bottom. He is there to be blamed when things get lost or when the boss blows up; and in that he serves a vital function as the world's safety valve. A boss without a boy is unthinkable. For while the greyhound can be satisfied with an electric hare, I do not think the boss will ever be satisfied with an electric boy, even one guaranteed not to whistle.

The Game is only the Half of it

One must view with perturbation, if not, indeed, with consternation, this modern tendency towards pulling down the old ramshackle terraces of our football stadia and replacing them with luxury stands of the 'Seating and Covered Accommodation for All' type of thing.

That old west terrace in Croke Park, for example, scene of many a tumultuous heave-ho-my-hearties in the old democratic sardine-packed days of the great Gaels of Ireland, The Men Whom God Made Mad, is now a monster luxury stand with luxury seats where presidents and bishops and archbishops and ambassadors are received in style and elegance. And across the Tolka river an exquisite little early-century period-piece of muck-and-timber terracing, down whose steep slopes doughty fellows used to hurtle and heave and kick each other in their hundreds in the great days of Drumcondra Football Club, is now a solid, comfortable, concrete stand whereon effete decadents sprawl in supine apathy.

One, as I say, must view all this with perturbation. This is the sort of thing that made the Roman Empire into what it had no business becoming. It makes football followers observers rather than participants. It gives rise to the modern heresies of The-Game's-The-Thingism and One-Team's-As-Good-As-Anotherism. It generates such terrible cults as Fair-Play-For-Umpireism. It substitutes the meagre judicial handclap for the generous partisan bellow. It leads on to Rugs-Over-The-Knees and, ultimately, to Hot-Water-Bottles-For-All.

I am myself an inhabitant—or denizen, if you will have it so—of the unreserved terraces, since the first day I learned at my father's knee to lisp maledictions at referees. Through the years I have crushed and scrambled with the lowest of the sporting low; from university undergraduates to Glasgow Rangers' supporters there is no segment of the underworld of sporting society that has not enjoyed its fair crack at my shin-bones, its due lean on my shoulders. And this much I have leared from my travails . . . a man who is not experiencing his ball game from a standing, or rather a sway-ing, position among his peers might just as well, for all the good it will do his soul, 'have stood in bed'.

For standing men are active; seated men are passive. The only thing that a man seated at a football game can do with himself is to look at the football, and that is a pretty thin form of entertainment most times. To the true sportsman the game is not, and never was intended to be, the whole thing. It is merely a component part; an excuse for all the narking, bellowing, reminiscing, shoulder-slapping and rib-poking that, combined, go to make up the healthy, open-air, citizens' sport of big-game-spectating.

On the free-and-easy unreserved terraces no man is an island. The heave which affecteth me affecteth the one in front of me even more so. But in the formal order of things which prevails in reserved stands, every man is an island. He is given his appointed place and there he must abide to the bitter end; for any attempt on his part to stand up will bring down upon his head that awful ululation: '*SIT DOWN IN FRONT OWER THAT* . . .'

What is to become of the characters of the unreserved terraces; the flowers of malice and wit that must needs perish without the sustenance of the cheer-ful rabble? What of the well-loved familiars? The tall guy who is always get-ting cursed by the crowd; the small guy who is always cursing the crowd; the man who won't take off his hat; the bewildered little woman who must, one presumes, be somebody's mother; the chap who obligingly faints and gives everyone a high old time sliding him down on a carpet of upraised arms; the non-stop narker who is always expecting something dreadful to happen, and grimly determined to be there when it does . . .

. . . 'It's a disgrace, that's wha' it is, the number a people that's been let in; it's on-huming. ON-HUMING; yez'd think we wus cattles or somethin'. Sup-posin', I MEAN JEST SUPPOSIN' SOMETHIN' WUS TO HAPPEN. Wha' chances has anny of us? Why, we'd be murthured. YIS MURTHURED. Lookit wha' happened thar in Itly last year. Lookit them misfawrtnit chislers over thar under the wall, I ask yez wha' chances has them misfawrtnit chislers if annythin' was to happen to that wall? But wha' do THAT CROWD IN THAR care about you or me or them misfawrtnit chislers! THAT CROWD IN THAR isn't out for you or me THAT CROWD IN THAR IS ONEY OUT FOR THEIRSELVES . . .'

Perhaps that is the authentic voice of the terraces: The nark; the jeremiad of those without the law. For we of the terraces are the voice of disorder, and now THAT CROWD IN THAR are extending their order and their 'seated and covered accommodation' to seat, cover and civilise us—and make us pay double for the privilege.

What? Just to sit alone in one's ivory tower, high above the blood and sand of the arena, clapping one's frozen hands and commenting *sanely* on the progress of the play?

Ah, no! That is no way to go to a ball game. Sure a man might as well be PLAYING in the thing for all the fun he could get out of that.

Myself and the Critics

There were some thirty minutes to go before closing-time, so, turning from the newspaper building, I entered one of its licensed annexes. I ordered a pint, and I opened the long brown envelope for a final reading of the piece which I was about to contribute.

I was feeling pretty superior about it. Lengthy rolling periods, well-dressed well-placed adjectives; Chestertonian, I reflected, if not indeed Bellocian; wit, paradox, and—why not admit it?—profundity as well. That splendid opening sentence for example: One hundred and twenty words, fifteen commas, four semi-colons, one colon, and two hyphenated phrases. Classy, to say the very least . . .

'The hard man hisself,' a voice broke in on my complacent dreams, 'is that another writings ye have there wid ye?'

'Nothing that would interest you at all,' I answered hurriedly. 'Different kind of thing altogether to what I usually do . . . Literary, sort of, if you know what I mean . . .'

But the voice continued unabashed, and I finally had to admit the company of my old friend, sometimes reader, and frequent supplier of printable and unprintable anecdote, Methuselah. He was in company with an even more venerable ancient.

'His nibs hyar,' explained Methusaleh to the Venerable One, 'is a rare dab hand with the pen.'

The Venerable One had the cold eye and the tight lip of the congenital iconoclast. He looked at me with obvious distaste. 'An amatewer writer, is it?' he sneered.

It was squelch or be squelched. 'Ectually,' I spoke in superior tones, 'ectually I get paid for it.'

It was the wrong answer. The Venerable One turned his head to the bar and bayed. 'Ye git paid for it, hah! An' will ye tell me wan thing, Will ye tell me isn't it a tarrible thing for men to be coming inta a boozer for a jar an' them men talkin' words, and another man to be writing down them words an' gettin' paid for it?'

He had a point there, of course, and I should have settled the matter with a courteous 'What'll you have on the strength of it?' But the ringing of my deep-toned adjectives was still in my head. Strewth! Was Dublin's up-and-coming man of letters to flee from a tight lip and a cold eye?

'It's a damm sight easier for you to talk them than for me to write them,' I bleated to the bar.

It was my second mistake. For the trouble about arguing with old-timers is that no matter how many subjects you beat them on they can always come back at you with their own special, unique subject of old times.

He allowed me a few minutes' swagger. Then he came at me. 'I suppose that yew,' he queried, 'being as ye are an amateur writer an' all that, would have a great knowledge of Dublin?'

I saw my danger and, downing my pint, I rose for what was intended to be a swift tactical retreat. But even as I did so my old friend Methuselah, in his enthusiasm, unwittingly stabbed me in the back.

'Sairtindly he has,' declared Methuselah, 'why the man is a walking bewk of this town.'

The Venerable One struck. "Fair enough, me walkin' bewk.' he roared. 'Can ye stand yer ground and answer a few queskins of Dublin history?'

'Sairtindly he can,' enthused my admirer and patron. 'Ask him any queskins ye can think of.'

The Venerable One winked at his friends in the bar. 'What,' he demanded, 'was channel twist?'

Methuselah looked at me expectantly. I looked at the floor despondently. The Venerable One looked at the bar triumphantly. 'Thar y'are,' he roared, 'his nibs hyar never had to stand outside a Corless's or wan of them eatin' houses waiting for the nobs to drop their cigar butts in the gutter so that he could pick them up and roll the tabaccy for a fill. That was channel twist, son; the only twist that many a pewer man could afford in them days.'

Even before I had recovered from the first round he had come at me for the second. 'Whar an' what was the stand-up lodgin?'

Again it was the round to him. These things may be history, but my bewks never treated them as such. In fact my bewks had never treated of them at all. How was I to know that the stand-up-lodgin' was 'round thar be Poolbeg Street', and that you called it the stand-up-lodgin' because when the beds were full you took your place for the night in a long line with other bedless

A man of adamantine facts

ones, your head supported on a rope running under your chin, and when they wanted to wake you in the morning they just cut the rope and let you bounce off the floor.

The terrible minutes passed by to the curfew hour, while the fearful 'queskins' rattled across the bar at me. Alone I stood, a man of flaccid adjectives opposed to men of adamantine facts. The landlord called for time, and the Venerable One rose to go. 'Stick around sonny,' he invited, 'an' we'el larn ye yet . . .' Deflated I watched him go, my strings of adjectives shattered like strings of beads. What does he of Dublin know who only Gilbert knows?

Methuselah, in tactful sympathy, reached for the long brown envelope. 'What's it all about anyway,' he asked, and faced with the query I suddenly realised that it did not seem to be about anything in particular. He sighed gustily as he finished reading. 'Very elegint indeed,' he declared. Then he looked carefully at some distant point in the ceiling. 'And anyway, sure I mean to say, they'd be sure not to blow ye out on it, just-in-case-ye-turned-up-with-something-dacent-the next-time.'

I read it again, a cold doubt seeping through the remnants of my enthusiasm . . . Wit, was it? Or was it whimsy? Profundity, was it? Or was it platitude? Paradox was it? Or was it piffle?

Near the junction of O'Connell Street and Henry Street there is a rubbish-box attached to a lamp standard. In the rubbish-box reposes, for all I know, a masterpiece in a long brown envelope. If you, sir or madam, happen across it there, or if it should happen to blow against your feet from off some slobland, pray use it as you see fit. Keep it for some local debating society, if you wish; as I remember it could be used to prove or disprove almost anything. It may even be that it could create a sensation for you.

I do not know. I do not want to know. I never want to see it again.

Epilogue

À la Recherche du Tom Perdu

Here be ghosts

It was Dublin; it was the fifties; and if it was not exactly the best of times it was far, far away from being the worst of times.

Thousands and thousands of people not alone lived in inner Dublin then; they enjoyed living there. The hard times of the thirties and the forties were on the way out, and at long last there were a few shillings stirring. Not to Marbella or Miami did the neighbours go on the holliers, but the Isle of Man and Blackpool were coming within the reach of most of us, and faint rumours of strange exotic foreign places like Kerry and Clare and Galway were coming to the ears of the chislers.

As you walked the Dublin streets of the fifties you became aware of a fairly amiable (most times) conglomeration of separate quarters, each with a certain faintly defined but sure hierarchical order of its own. Everybody seemed fairly easily ensconced in his own scene, unenvying of his neighbour. Yet the poet could and did share the same pub with the peasant, and no man had need of looking up, down, or askance at his fellow man.

On summer nights along those Summerhill streets where rows and rows of blind and shuttered houses now look down on empty shops and play grounds chislers would play in the sun; fish and chips would scent the air; oul' wans sitting in the windows of the tall old houses taking the sunshine would give and receive the news. Television was to be observed here and there, but not, as of yet, everywhere. So one moved homewards at an easy pace, not having an urgent appointment with JR, The Late Show, Match of the Day, Parki, Panorama, The Royal Shakespeare, The London Philharmonic, The Top Twenty or Coronation Street.

Instead one stood and talked, and there was an immense amount of talk to be had for the price of a pint. Every pub had its own guru. Not all of them had names. Someone might be known to you merely as *Yer Man* or *The Quar Fella*. Somebody else was *The Head Case*. There was the majestic *Himself*, the tolerated *Gas Man*, and the most supreme guru of all, *Whar Would We Be Widout Him?*

But there were also public-house sages with real names on them. Patrick Kavanagh could be heard discoursing in MacDaid's of Harry Street on such esoteric subjects as professional boxing, the beauty of Ginger Rogers, or the dire state of Gaelic football in Ulster. Flann O'Brien could be heard in Neary's or the Scotch House on any subject known to man. Robert Marie Smyllie, Esq., editor of the *Irish Times* and chief autocrat of the breakfast table of the fifties, could be heard in the Palace Bar of Fleet Street, before he betook himself and his entire court across the road to the Pearl. Brendan Behan could be heard everywhere. God could be heard in his Heaven, and Adolescent People, except on Christmas Eve and New Year's Eve, could only be heard where they were meant to be heard, in Croke Park, or Dalymount, or the goings-on in the local hall.

Bliss, an inhabitant of the scene might truly have observed to himself, was it in that eve to be alive. To be middle-aged was very heaven.

But of course we inhabitants of that happy hour never did make that observation to ourselves for the very good reason that we none of us knew at the time that we were living at the end of the rainbow (indeed, one amongst, us witnessed, at the corner of South Anne Street and Grafton Street, Paddy Kavanagh and Flann O'Brien weeping on each other's shoulder, weeping because there were no more great Dublin characters around). The tumult and the shouting of the sixties was yet another world away. The Frankenstein monsters of the seventies had yet to be born. Conglomerates were gluey substances. An Office Block was something you bought the chisler for Christmas; a Merger was the Shels and the Bohs agreeing to share Dalymount Park; a Pill was a pain in the neck; an Ongoing Situation was a continuing pain in the neck; Relevant Scenarios At This Point In Time had not even reached a point in time; and any building over ten stories high was a municipal sensation. There was no talk of 'conservation' or 'preserving the environment' for the simple reason that nothing ever changed in the Dublin of those days. That it might change was unthought of; not even old Nosey could have made credible the fall of the Ballast Office.

In that leisurely and hospitable decade a shrewd ball-man could borrow a two-shilling piece (his entrance money as he would so call it) and entering a pub could reasonably hope, by good projection of his personality, wit, anecdotes and stock of blarney, to spend the evening as the guest of his peers. Nor was the ball-man despised for not having the readies in his own pocket; there was an unwritten law in Dublin then that the boon companion, like the labourer, was worthy of his hire.

It is not to say there there were more boon companions, be they writers, artists, poets, painters, gamblers, crooks or wasters to the square foot of Dublin pub space in those days than there are today. It just that they seemed to be so much more *manifest* in the fifties. Was it that they did not go home so much at nights? Was it, come to think of it, that not all had a home to go home to?

For all the companionship of the times, however, we did have certain local and geographical snobberies to which we lovingly clung. It was not the done thing for us plain, blunt sons of the northside to drink south of the river unless we had business with one of their specialised assets like the literary folk of MacDaid's of Harry Street, the theatre folk of Neary's in Chatham Street, or the public house singing folk in any pub along Camden Street.

And it certainly was not the customary thing for any snooty southsider to drink north of the river unless he was going to a dress dance in the Gresham or the Metropole, or had hopes of selling a play to Radio Eireann in Gerry O'Dwyer's pub in Moore Street, where in those days you betook yourself, if you wanted to sell a play to Radio Eireann.

So we sat and drank inexpensive pints in affable, uncrowded pubs where the barmen had ample time to discuss the match of the week-end, the pint came slowly from the cellar and the boss was nearly always good for a loan. We had darts, and rings, and question-time contests, and weighty discussions on the state of the nation. And if any prophet had entered one of our Nirvanas to tell us that most of us would live to see the day when a pound note could not purchase two pints of stout and a barman would not have time to discuss the horses, the dogs or the football with his customers we would have had him committed as a lunatic, if not indeed prosecuted as a disturber of the peace.

Now, marooned in the jet-set eighties, we bewildered survivors of the fifties wonder as we look around—whenever we get time to look around us . . . Has it all vanished; or is it still lying around somewhere and have we just lost track of it? Certainly the voice of the Abbey Street orator is no longer heard in the land. The *sin-gers* of the old musical pubs are being stood down in favour of professional cabaret artistes. The accents of Lancashire or Glasgow are heard but rarely in the boozers, and the sacred booze itself is no longer being slowly savoured by sages in meditation bent, but rather being gulped down the hatches of insatiable stomachs as though it were in danger of drying out overnight. The old Queen's Theatre, where used to dwell the Abbey players in temporary exile, has become a faceless home for functionaries. The rococo Capitol Theatre of Princes Street and its remarkable neighbour, the Metropole complex, where on snowy winter days you could breakfast at 9 a.m., crash a film press show at 10 a.m. have a pre-prandial drink at 12.30 p.m., follow with lunch at 1 p.m., go to the cinema at 2 p.m., have your tea at 6 p.m., read your newspaper over a few drinks until the ballroom opened at 8 p.m., collect a fair lady during the course of the dancing and then go down with her to the cellars for wine, supper and a cabaret which went on until the late hours of the morning without once having stuck your nose into the midwinter airs of Dublin, are now combined into a giant retail store where you can buy anything other than a pint.

True the Olympia Theatre has been saved once again, if not for the musical hall at least for the live shows, and the pint of stout has returned to its ancestral bars. But changed too is the pint, its practices and its practitioners. No longer pulled slowly from the wood, but now out of uniform metal casks, its tendency is to come out much the same in every house, and this leaves little room for the exercise of the pintman's critical faculties. How can you develop arguments about the relative qualities of pints that look alike as guardsmen on parade? Where do you go to nark about a bad pint? To what ancient tavern do you travel to savour the super pint? Even the pubs themselves have changed. The old seemly and decorous interior in shades of brown and mahogany has been engulfed by the insidious creeping influence of the carpeted lounge.

Even so we eccentric nostalgics still go searching for the perfect pint and its times. Yesterday's men, in our long overcoats and short back-and-sides, shrinking from unisex and long hair styles and discos and cabarets and the new glitterati of the gossip columns, you can behold us striding down North King Street to where an old spit-and-sawdust awaits us in Stoneybatter; belting out to Parkgate Street on the Liffey where we can still drink in the surround of marble and mahogany; skulking along Poolbeg Street to where in fuscous, seemly shades we conjure up visions of long-gone artistes from the Tivoli and the Royal; searching in bewildered fashion back of Thomas Street for another old marble-and-mahogany home that nobody told us had vanished.

In such places—if you know where to find such places—you will find us relics of the fifties. We only go there at the quiet times, for the young mods of the eighties are tending to adopt them too, and though we do not grudge them the pleasure of it we must preserve our dignity, we must keep ourselves to ourselves. We must be talking to our friends, and if you see us do not interrupt us; do not intrude on what looks like men talking to themselves.

For Here Be Ghosts.

Giving and receiving the news